PREFACE

In a Foreword to the first volume of Discovering Classical Music, the late Sir Charles Groves wrote the following words.

> Here is a book written by a very experienced music-lover for the encouragement of newcomers to the wonderful world of classical music.
>
> In his introduction the author has made a convincing case for writing the book; how successful has he been? He had first of all to decide whether to write a 'flip-through' guide to a large selection from a great number of composers, or to write at some length about a carefully considered few: choosing the latter of course, he lays himself open to criticism of his choice. There can be little argument about that precious handful of giants in the arts and, for the rest, personal judgement is paramount. Ian Christians emerges as a man of strong opinions, and some musicians might have frustration with his choice, but in the Introduction he explains his plan lucidly and convincingly.
>
> His 'potted biographies' are just the things for new listeners who will not want to be put off by too much specialised jargon, and bearing in mind that he aims to present his subjects as 'human' they are done with taste. He rightly stresses that the music he writes about is easily accessible to newcomers and he does his best to blow away the mists of snobbery and elitism which unfairly surrounds classical music.
>
> I find that each composer is given a well-selected list from his works so that an enquiring mind may know where to start and continue a search for experience in listening to classical music for the first time: with such an ocean of material to choose from, many people are bewildered and discouraged from dipping a toe in the water.
>
> I enjoyed reading this book and I recommend it whole-heartedly to new music-lovers everywhere.

In Discovering Classical Music 4 the choice of composers is extended further.

The Author

Ian Christians now spends his time as an author and publisher; a business mentor working with young entrepreneurs in London; running his Orpheus & Bacchus Music and Wine Festivals in France (orpheusandbacchus.com); and the luxury holiday homes (specialvillas.com) that he and his wife own near Bordeaux.

Author's Acknowledgements

Again my thanks to my designer, Tim Guy; my editor Elizabeth Cruickshank; my photo-typesetter, Chris Cardell-Williams; my artist George Israel, and of course my wife Sharon. Again my apologies to my series readers for being late with this volume – I will try to do better for future volumes. The Barbican Music Library in London has been a superb source.

Sources: primary sources of information on composers have included: *Henry Purcell* by Robert King (Thames and Hudson); *Weber* by Anthony Friese-Greene (Omnibus Press); *Robert Schumann* by John Daverio (Oxford University Press); *Franz Liszt* by Alan Walker (Faber & Faber); *Gabriel Fauré, His life through his letters* by Jean-Michel Nectoux (Marion Boyars); *Maurice Ravel* by Gerald Larner (Phaidon); *Belá Bartók* by Kenneth Chalmers, (Phaidon); *Benjamin Britten* by Humphrey Carpenter (Faber & Faber); *Shostakovich – A life remembered* by Elizabeth Wilson, (Faber & Faber). To these and others who have written on and researched the lives of the composers I am much in debt. Any errors of interpretation or fact are my responsibility.

Discovering
CLASSICAL
MUSIC

4

IAN CHRISTIANS

This book is dedicated to Jean, Barbara, Felix and George, new family in the year 2000.

Published by DCM Publications.

Cover and book design by Timothy Guy Design, Truro, Cornwall.

Phototypeset in 10/12pt Bembo by Carliam Artwork, Potters Bar, Herts.

Printed by Biddles Limited, Guildford, Surrey.

ISBN 0–9518301–5–5

DCM Publications

1 Hay's Court, 133 Rotherhithe Street, London SE16 4NF

CONTENTS

INTRODUCTION

DISCOVERING MORE BURIED TREASURE

*W*hen I started writing *Discovering Classical Music* my objective was to write just one book. I chose a mix of the greatest composers, the most popular composers and a couple of my favourites. But there was such a demand for more composers that a whole series evolved. My objective became to present forty composers in four volumes and this I have now achieved.

Whilst all the composers in *Volume 4* are acknowledged masters I have yet again come across little-known music that is an absolute delight. I have come to the conclusion that there are many more composers whom I would enjoy introducing to you in a similar fashion.

In the Appendix I have mapped out the composers for the next four planned volumes. If and when I have finished the last of these, my experience suggests that I will probably announce a further four volumes!

We live in a critical age and one where the competition for our leisure time gets ever fiercer. If few composers can match the genius of Bach, Mozart, Beethoven or Schubert (who have between them written enough for a lifetime of music), we can still be open to – and delighted by - some marvellous works written by their fellow craftsmen.

Help is definitely on the way. Serious recording companies are finding the case for recording the music of the less well-known composers is increasingly attractive compared to adding to the hundreds of recordings of a Beethoven symphony. Technology is helping too, so that hopefully many rare operas will eventually be captured in stunning sound and vision on DVD for a global market of afficionados and the curious.

Happy discoveries!

Henry Purcell

1

PURCELL

Purcell *His Life*

*A*s best can be guessed Henry Purcell was born in 1659 in London, England, the second of three sons. His father and mother were either Thomas and Katherine Purcell or Thomas' brother Henry and his wife Elizabeth Purcell. Both Thomas and Henry were top professional musicians who had been trained as choristers at St.George's Chapel, Windsor Castle. Young Henry was born into one of England's most turbulent periods. Charles I had been executed in 1649 and Oliver Cromwell had disbanded the Court and its musicians but his Commonwealth was now under threat. Theatre performances and public concerts had also been banned by Cromwell so life had been difficult for the Purcell brothers.

The restoration of the monarchy and return of the music-loving Protestant Charles II was the start of better times. Both brothers were appointed to the reformed Chapel Royal, initially as singers but soon in more exalted positions. Henry was given the task of creating a new choir for Westminster Abbey before becoming lutenist, but he died in August 1664 at the age of 40. From then on Thomas was the head of the family. The next year the Plague killed a third of London's population. The Court musicians and their families followed the Royal Court and moved first to Windsor, then for a time to the West Country. The following year, 1666, brought the Great Fire of London and war with the Dutch.

The young Purcell joined the Chapel Royal choir as a treble around the age of eight and lived at Whitehall in London. The choristers received an extensive musical education, including composing, and the first group of choristers produced some notable composers including John Blow. There is a story that Henry Purcell composed an ode for the 40th birthday of Charles II in 1670. Life as a chorister was hard work but exciting, with performances given at theatres as well as royal palaces outside London.

Purcell's voice broke when he was fourteen and he had to leave the choir. A warrant dated June 10, 1673, appointed him to a new unpaid position. It read:

> *"To admit Henry Purcell in the place of keeper, maker, mender, repayrer and tuner of the regalls, organs, virginalls, flutes and recorders and all other kind of wind instruments whatsoever, in ordinary, without fee, to his Majesty, and assistant to John Hingston, and upon the death or other avoydance of the latter, to come in ordinary with fee."*

Purcell did not starve because his family could provide for him. However, matters improved three months later when he was awarded £30 per annum – when he received it was another matter because the Exchequer was a notoriously slow payer, sometimes years in arrears! His position was an ideal one for understanding the instruments of an orchestra and he continued to receive lessons. In 1676 Matthew Locke, who was one of Purcell's teachers, was appointed Master of the King's Music along with John Blow. When he died a year later Purcell composed an ode *"On the death of his Worthy Friend"*, and was promoted to succeed him but with the title of Composer in Ordinary for the Violins.

For such a young musician to be appointed to this post said much for his talent, although questions of nepotism must have been raised because amongst his numerous roles Thomas Purcell was the other orchestral composer. Purcell's new position demanded that he composed for, directed and managed the orchestra for Court and theatre perform-ances. A key requirement was to compose odes for occasions such as the King's birthday and his return from periods away from London.

Purcell was now in a position of prominence and John Playford, London's leading music publisher, included some of his songs in a collection printed in 1679. Purcell had to carry out his work in difficult political times. Charles II contracted pneumonia and his Catholic brother James returned from Belgium, creating a period of instability. To make more money Purcell gave music lessons and took on the position of Organist at Westminster Abbey, succeeding his teacher John Blow. This ensured that he avoided the travel to the King's other palaces at Windsor and Hampton Court and was thus able to dedicate more time to composition.

Purcell's range of music broadened steadily with commercial opportunities expanding as more theatres and music rooms opened. There was a thriving market for his popular songs too, many highly bawdy as was typical of the time. During his travels he met Frances Pieters, whose family owned an eating house in Southwark, on the south side of the River Thames. Frances's father was Flemish but had settled in London and taken English citizenship.

The couple married in 1680 and Purcell bought a small house in Westminster, ideal for his work. A son, Henry, was born in July 1681 but died a few days later. Thomas Purcell fell ill and died the following summer, and Frances gave birth to another son, John Baptista, in August 1682, only for him to die two months later – these were sad times for the Purcells.

Driven by the example of the Italian composer Corelli, Purcell published a set of 12 string sonatas in 1683 and dedicated them to Charles II. The handsome set included a likeness of the composer and an introduction by him – a rare sense of the real man. It ends *"The Author has no more to add but his hearty wishes that his Book may fall into no other hands but theirs with Musical Souls about them; for he is willing to flatter himself into a belief that with Such his labours will seem neither unpleasant, nor unprofitable."*

The same year saw the completion of the *Ode to St. Cecilia*, one of Purcell's best known works. At the end of 1683 Hingston died and Purcell was appointed to his position as keeper of the King's Instruments, as in the original warrant. This responsibility was arduous in a desperately cold winter, but the next year saw the creation of some of his best anthems. Towards the end of the year the Purcells moved to a larger house even closer to the Abbey.

The autumn welcome ode *From Those Serene and Rapturous Joys* was to be the last that Purcell wrote for Charles II, who died the following February after having last rites administered by a Catholic priest. All the children of Charles II were illegitimate so the crown fell to his brother James. Purcell played a major role in the coronation of James II in Westminster Abbey and several of his anthems were played. Under the new Catholic monarch there was, regrettably, little chance of a Protestant providing church music, but secular music such as the *Welcome Odes* was still commissioned and James II appointed Purcell as

Harpsichordist in 1685. However the underlying hostility towards Protestants often took the form of non-payment of salary and by 1687 Purcell was owed two years' pay.

Frances gave birth to another son in June, again named Henry, and again the baby didn't survive, dying three months later. She quickly became pregnant again and gave birth in May 1688 to a daughter who enjoyed good health. Because Purcell's official work load was relatively light, he started on a new project, the opera *Dido and Aeneas*, with the poet Nahum Tate, later appointed Poet Laureate. It was written for Josia Priest's School for Young Gentlewomen in Chelsea. The reign of James II came to an end in December 1688. His daughter Mary, a Protestant, was married to William of Orange who arrived back in England at the head of a small army. James II's army disintegrated and he fled to Ireland to regroup, leaving Mary and William to be offered the crown jointly in February 1689.

In these dramatic times Purcell's future was at first uncertain but his position was confirmed in April. He participated in the Coronation ceremony but did not write any new works for it. Shortly afterwards he unveiled for the new Queen's 27th birthday the first of a number of exceptional odes. *Dido and Aeneas* had its premiere and its success led to more opportunities to write theatre music, first of all *Dioclesian*, a play with remarkable stage effects for the time. In September 1689 Frances Purcell at last gave birth to a healthy son, Edward.

1691 saw Purcell working with the poet Dryden on a new opera, *King Arthur*. It was a great success and ran for many months. Music for *The Fairy Queen*, based on Shakespeare's *Midsummer Night's Dream*, was composed the following year. For St. Cecilia's Day celebrations Purcell composed the celebrated *Hail, Bright Cecilia*.

Frances Purcell gave birth to another daughter, Mary, in December 1693 and the family was complete. A month later Purcell had the opportunity to travel to Dublin, for the premiere of an ode commissioned to celebrate the centenary of Trinity College, but he made his excuses. In April he provided *Come Ye Sons of Art Away* for Queen Mary's birthday. The following year the St. Cecilia celebrations launched the *Te Deum* and *Jubilate*, both using a full orchestra for the first time.

Queen Mary died in December 1694 as the result of a smallpox epidemic that had started in the summer. Her popularity required a state funeral that had to be delayed for three months. Purcell composed much of the music for this big occasion. Much of his time afterwards was spent on music for the theatre, for which his major work was *The Indian Queen*.

At this stage in his life everything pointed to a long and celebrated career, but disaster struck. Although the circumstances, like much of Purcell's life, are not clear, it seems that he contracted an infection in November 1695 and his condition deteriorated dramatically. He died on the eve of St. Cecilia's Day, November 21. Purcell's funeral took place in Westminster Abbey, accompanied by the music he had written for the funeral of Queen Mary. He was afforded the honour of being buried in the Abbey at the foot of the organ. Shortly afterwards there was a memorial concert for which Purcell's colleagues wrote odes of homage. That of the composer Henry Hall concluded with the words:

> *"Sometimes a Hero in an age appears*
> *But Once a Purcell in a Thousand Years"*

Purcell *The person*

Purcell had a fresh face with a prominent nose and fair skin. He was highly sociable and liked to spend time in coffee and drinking houses with friends, of whom he had many. He mixed easily at all levels of society, although the status of a musician was rather low at the time.

He was a strong family person although it is likely that he strayed during his marriage, such were the temptations in 17th century London. Certainly he was conservative in his daily life, and did not travel far from London, resisting opportunities to visit other countries and to experience different musical cultures. He was an honest man who dealt fairly with others and had the respect of fellow musicians.

He was an innovator in music and highly industrious and productive, well able to turn out great masterpieces to order and to deadlines.

7

Purcell *His Music*

Welcome to the world of music in the seventeenth century as practised by one whom many rate as the greatest English composer. Being transported to this era, particularly with period instruments, is a great experience.

Odes

The numerous Royal, Ceremonial and Welcome Odes represent perhaps the greatest of Purcell's music, written in many cases for the full force of chorus and orchestra. Further, at about twenty minutes length, they are nicely concentrated, but full of variety provided by the different combinations of voices and chorus. I commend them to you.

Twenty-four have survived. Six celebrate various birthdays of Queen Mary (1689 – 1694), nine welcome royalty, four celebrate St. Cecilia's Day, and the remainder are occasion specific. They are a great treasure, largely and unjustifiably neglected. Perhaps this is because the texts often leave a lot to be desired and can be appallingly obsequious to the Royal family and the aristocracy!

Ode on St. Cecilia's Day opens with an extended and formidable *Overture* for an orchestra that includes oboes, recorders, trumpets and timpani. *Hail Bright Cecilia* is introduced by a bass before the chorus arrives in full voice. Countertenors, tenors and basses take solo roles in the following sections. *Soul of the World* is a mighty centrepiece, a thrilling and majestic chorus. *Wondrous Machine* is a hypnotic bass solo with a lovely woodwind accompaniment and after this eulogy for the organ other instruments are considered in solos. The fife (with trumpet and timpani) is particularly effective before the opening chorus returns for a thrilling conclusion, with superb antiphonal effects.

Now does the glorious day appear (1689 birthday of Queen Mary) has strings alone for accompaniment. The chorus opens with the basses, followed by ascending sections of the chorus. The highlight is *By Beauteous softness*, for alto, its climax at *She with such sweetness*, its conclusion a long passage for strings. A rousing choral conclusion ends with lovely resonances on the thrice-repeated final word "ring".

Arise My Muse (1690 birthday of Queen Mary) is unusual in having an excellent libretto. The orchestra includes recorders, oboes and trumpets and the opening is uplifting with dominant trumpet fanfares. *Ye sons of music raise your voices high* is a classic example of a brilliant chorus, jaunty, joyful and tuneful. The alto voice has two inspired solos, *See how the glitt'ring ruler of the day* and *But ah, I see Eusebia drowned in tears*, the latter supported by the added pathos of the recorders. The work concludes with the choral plea *Go on, great Prince, go on*.

Come ye sons of Art, away (the 1694 offering for the birthday of Queen Mary) is perhaps the most famous of Purcell's odes. His creativity took full advantage of a text that had plenty of references to music and musical instruments. The concluding adagio of the opening *Symphony* is particularly moving, before we are straight into the title song performed by alto voice, and *To celebrate this triumphant day*, resoundingly reinforced by the chorus. Next we have *Sound the trumpet*, an alto duet, where voices brilliantly mimic the instruments, before the opening chorus returns to round off the duet. Next we move to the intimate and ecstatic *Strike the viol*, solo instruments around the alto. The orchestral ritornello (an extended closing) is ravishing; two recorders and strings provide a feather-soft sound. In *Bid the virtues* a soprano voice partners an oboe to superb effect. Finally we conclude with a joyful celebration in the closing number, chorus, trumpets and timpani exultant. Wow!

Welcome, viceregent of the mighty King was Purcell's first ode, written when he was just 21 for the return of King Charles II to London in September 1680. Purcell superimposes the opening chorus over the second section of the opening *Symphony*. *But your blest presence now* is a witty, jaunty chorus followed by a lovely string ritornello. The chorus echoes the tenor throughout the next passage. Two sopranos bring freshness and light to *When the Summer, in his glory*. The delightful *Music, the food of love* is given to the tenor solo and chorus, before a ritornello precedes the final chorus, concluding with the words *God save the King*.

Welcome to all the Pleasures (St. Cecilia's Day 1683) is smaller in scale, the orchestra being composed of strings and organ only. The alto voice is given the moving *Here the Deities approve*, the tenor sings *Beauty, thou scene of love*. A particularly radiant song, for two sopranos and bass, is *While joys celestial their bright souls invade*. The closing chorus is highly original, dying away to the words *Iô Cecilia* handed down from sopranos to basses.

The *Funeral Music for Queen Mary* consists of two resonant pieces for brass either side of a short anthem. Short it may be, but it is also profound, portraying vividly the grief of the occasion.

Stage Works

Dido and Aeneas is a chamber opera concerning the love of Dido, Queen of Carthage, for Aeneas, who deserts her. The inclusion of a Sorceress and Enchantresses adds spice to the story. The opening of the *Overture* sets a melancholy mood but the music quickly gives way to liveliness. The chorus plays an important part in this fast-moving opera, with passages of commentary throughout. The music is delightful, the solos tend to be slow but choruses such as *When monarchs unite* are invigorating. *Fear no danger* for Dido's sister Belinda and chorus gorgeously gives way to an evocative dance, taking us back over 300 years. *Act 1* ends with the delights of the chorus and *Triumphing Dance*. The *Echo Chorus* and *Echo Dance of the Furies* create superb effects in *Act 2*. *Act 3* commences with a *Sailor's Chorus* and *Dance* but everything builds to Dido's famous lament, *When I am laid in earth*. A sad chorus and dance conclude this concise masterpiece.

King Arthur was not an opera as such, as it contains spoken dialogue and dances which was the preference of English audiences at the time. (Sometimes it is referred to as a semi-opera.) The plot has been realistically described as *"a fantastic jumble"*, so let us concentrate on the music. The *Overture* is striking, eventually trumpet fanfares launch the action. In *Act 1* the moving chorus *Brave Souls* stands out, along with *Come if you dare*. In *Act 2* there are glorious effects from two spirit choruses *Hither this way*. In *Act 3* Purcell creates an extraordinary frost scene with tremolando strings and rising and falling progressions, a perfect effect depicting Genius arising from beds of everlasting snow. *Act 4* opens with the seductive *Sirens' song* and continues with the centrepiece, the superb tenor aria, *How happy the lover* in which the chorus has a major part. *Act 5* contains a succession of memorable numbers, opening with *Ye Blust'ring Brethren*, a song with brilliant accompaniment, sandwiched between great trumpet displays. Later comes the patriotic *Fairest Isle, all Isles Excelling* and the love dialogue *You say,'Tis love creates the Pain*. *King Arthur* ends with a triumphant jingoistic chorus *Our Natives not alone appear* and a *Chaconne*.

The Indian Queen is a similar entertainment and has another bizarre plot with which I shall not bother you. The music is another matter. There are a number of orchestral numbers, an impressive *Overture*, a spectacular *Trumpet Overture*, a *Dance* and two *Symphonies*. The chorus *We the spirits of the air* is a delightful gavotte and *I attempt from love's sickness to fly in vain* is justly well known amongst Purcell's songs. This pantechnicon of delights concludes with an uplifting chorus.

Each of the five acts of *The Fairy Queen* includes a masque which is the focus for most of the music of the piece. It is entertaining and full of comedy, as demonstrated in the *Scene of the Drunken Poet*. In *Act 2* we have a great sequence of songs, *Night, Mystery, Secresie* (with a lovely recorder accompaniment) and *Sleep* (a remarkable hushed piece with chorus). *Act 3* includes *If love's a Sweet passion* and *Ye Gentle Spirits of the Air*, both serious songs. A formidable *Symphony* opens the masque in *Act 4*, which celebrates Oberon's birthday. The choruses are joyful, the fanfares for the entry of Phoebus are triumphant, and the songs that represent the seasons highly effective – *Winter* is particularly bleak. The masque of *Act 5* is exotic, the scene a Chinese garden, and *The Fairy Queen* ends with a *Chaconne* and a rousing trio and Chorus.

Anthems

Purcell's anthems are amongst the most appealing of his works. Short, with full chorus and soloists, and sometimes orchestral accompaniment, they give a clear demonstration of his genius.

The opening of *O Lord God of hosts, (Z37)* each part entering in turn, is inspired, Purcell writing for eight parts. Soon there is a fine rhythmic section at *Thou hast made us a very strife. Remember not, Lord, our offences (Z50)* is a profound and intense gem.

I was glad was performed at the coronation of James II in 1685. At the concluding *Glory be to the Father* Purcell breaks into "*a dazzling display of counterpoint*".

My heart is inditing (Z30) concluded the same ceremony. It is a wonderfully sonorous work, appropriately uplifting. Soloists narrate part of the text, and the orchestra has a substantial part alone, the contrast allowing the chorus to make a powerful impact. The final *Allelujahs* are thrilling.

11

Man that is born of a woman (Z30) from the Burial Service is appropriately restrained, creating a mood of consolation. *Thou knowest, Lord* (Z58c) is a brief gem, noble and serene.

O sing unto the Lord a new song (Z34) has string accompaniment and is a great celebration. *They that go down to the sea in ships* (Z57) opens with an extended string section, followed by a substantial bass solo that plumbs the depths before being joined by a counter-tenor. The chorus only joins in for the peroration.

Praise the Lord, O Jerusalem (Z46) builds to a lively and appropriately exalted climax, *Allelujahs* ringing out

Services

Purcell inevitably wrote much music for church services, here is a selection. The *Service in B flat* from the Evening Service contains a *Cantate Domino, Deus Miseratur, Magnificat* and *Nunc Dimittis*. The words are in English, the accompanying instrument is the organ and the effect is to lift the spirits.

The *Te Deum and Jubilate in D* was written for St. Cecilia's Day in 1694. It opens with celebratory trumpets, helping to create a splendid work, the rich solo and choral singing enhanced by the added brilliance of the trumpets. The *Jubilate*, in particular, attacks in a superbly rhythmic manner.

String Music

Viol consorts were the early equivalent of the string quartet and Purcell wrote numerous fantasies (up to seven parts) for these instruments just as they were going out of fashion. They are a fascinating reminder of a bygone age, a little like multi-instrument precursors of Bach's Cello Suites though with less variety, particularly of tempo, so that they are best heard in small doses.

Keyboard

Purcell wrote eight *Suites* for harpsichord. They are attractive works, which assist the Purcell lover to appreciate the composer fully.

Songs

Purcell's songs are great entertainment, and the popular music of the day. Great tunes and a rousing chorus makes *Tis wine was made to rule the day* a great drinking song for all time. The witty *When the cock begins to crow* is written for alto, tenor and bass. The soprano and tenor voices in *How pleasant is this flowery plain* are gorgeously accompanied by two flutes. *Oh! What a scene does entertain my sight* has a flute accompanying soprano and bass voices. There are many more.

Chevalier Gluck

14

2

GLUCK

Gluck *His Life*

Christoph Willibald Gluck was born on July 2, 1714, in Erasback, a small village now in Northern Bavaria. Christoph was the first surviving child of Alexander Johann Gluck and his wife Anna, who were to have four further sons and two daughters. Alexander Gluck came from a family of foresters and on his appointment as forest-master to the Duchess Anna Maria of Tuscany the family moved to what is now Liberec in Bohemia, the first of several relocations as Alexander changed his employers.

As was usual in Bohemia, Gluck's education had a strong musical element. His schoolteacher gave him a grounding in several instruments and he quickly stood out from the other children. He became very proficient on the Jew's harp that he carried around with him. Alexander Gluck wanted his eldest son to carry on the family tradition in forestry but Gluck was determined to follow a career in music. At the age of 17 he left the family home to enrol at the faculty of Philosophy in the University of Prague. From 1731 to 1734 Gluck studied, taking on an organist's post to pay his way and experiencing the rich musical life of Prague where operas were particularly popular.

In 1734 it is believed that Gluck left Prague to go to Vienna. There he took a position with the Lobkowitz household for whom previous generations of his family had worked. He was successful in attracting some significant patrons for his performances, one of whom was a 65-year-old Milanese prince who, after marrying a 16-year-old girl, invited Gluck back to Milan.

Gluck's four-year period in Milan is shrouded in mystery. It is possible that he continued his musical education by taking lessons from Giovanni Battista Sammartini, but what is certain is that it was here that he composed his first opera *Artaserse* which was performed on Boxing

Day in 1741. Despite its innovative expressive style it was a great success. *Artaserse* was followed by *Demetrio* and *Demofoonte*. The latter opera was so well received, that after the famous castrato Giovanni Corestina performed in it in 1743, it was quickly taken up by a number of other Italian cities. The prolific Gluck wrote four further operas in 1744.

Early in 1745 Gluck left Milan and we know only that he arrived in Frankfurt in the autumn for the coronation celebrations of Emperor Francis I. Afterwards he moved on to London, probably persuaded by one of the agents regularly sent from the English capital to find singing talent in Italy. Gluck quickly composed *La caduta de' Giganti*, premiered in January 1746 at the Haymarket Theatre, and followed it two months later with *Artamene*.

It was inevitable that Gluck would meet Handel who dominated musical London at that time. When asked what sort of composer Gluck was, Handel responded *"He knows no more of contrapunto as mein cook, Waltz."* Handel's advice to Gluck after the premiere of *La caduta de' Giganti* was *"You have taken too much trouble with the opera but that is not needed here. For the English you must have something striking, which has its effect directly on the eardrums, and your opera will then be sure to please."* Gluck's addition of trombones to the choruses had an immediate beneficial effect!

Gluck was successful in London and was awarded two benefit concerts in April 1746. Part of the announcement read: *"Particularly he will play a Concerto upon Twenty-six Drinking Glasses, tuned with Spring-Water, accompanied with the whole Band, being a new instrument of his own invention; upon which he performs whatever may be done on a Violin or Harpsichord; and therefore hopes to satisfy the Curious as well as the Lovers of Musick."*

Gluck left London shortly afterwards, never to return. Within a year he was working with a travelling opera company led by Pietro Mingotti whom he had met in Frankfurt. *Le nozze d'Ercole e d'Ebe* was composed to celebrate a double royal wedding celebration in Dresden between the Bavarian and Saxon Royal Houses. It is likely that he met the Austrian ambassador to Saxony, Prince Nikolaus Esterházy, because his next opera, *La Semiramide*, was written for the reopening of the Burgtheater in Vienna in May 1748. Such was its reception that it was performed 26 times over the following two months. The poet Metastasio, whose works were the basis for many opera libretti including *La Semiramide*, described the music as *"ultra-barbaric and intolerable"*.

Hamburg was Gluck's next destination and he joined Mingotti's troupe there in August 1748. Gluck was appointed Kappellmeister of the Hamburg Theatre soon afterwards. He took one of the singers as his mistress and fell seriously ill, probably with syphilis. Recovering, Gluck next composed *La contessa de'numi* for the Danish Royal Court in Copenhagen. He took the opportunity presented by his visit to give two concerts which included performances on his glass-harmonica. Next he switched to another troupe, that of Giovanni Battista Locatelli for whom he composed *Ezio* for Prague in December 1749.

Sometime between 1748 and 1750 Gluck met Maria Anna Bergin, the daughter of the wealthy Viennese merchant, Joseph Bergin. Romance blossomed but Marianne (as she was known) was forbidden by her father from marrying Gluck. Fortunately for the composer, Joseph died, leaving Marianne a wealthy woman and on September 15, 1751, Gluck and Marianne married.

Although the couple settled in Vienna Gluck was soon off on his travels, composing *Issipile* for the Locatelli troupe where he became Director. In March 1752 he received a commission from the Teatro San Carlo in Naples. Although he was initially requested to compose for the libretto of *Arsace*, he persuaded the impresario to give him *La Clemenza di Tito* instead. One of the arias, "*Se mai senti spirarti sul volto*", written for the famous castrato Caffarelli, became popular throughout Italy.

Gluck's reputation in Naples led to an appointment in 1753 with Prince Joseph Friedrich von Sachsen-Hildberghausen in Vienna as concert-master of his exceptional orchestra. The following year Gluck wrote *Le Cinesi* for an Imperial visit to Prince Joseph Friedrich's summer residence. No expense was spared on the production and the visit was a great success. Gluck received a gold snuff box containing 100 ducats and thus began an important relationship with the Imperial Court that was to result in a series of commissions for Imperial celebrations.

Towards the end of 1755 Gluck visited Rome to write *Antigono* for the Teatro di Torre Argentina. He was acclaimed in the city and became a Knight of the Golden Spur, a papal honour. From then on Gluck used the title Chevalier. On his return to Vienna he was appointed Court

Composer. Opéra-comique had become fashionable in Vienna as a result of performances imported directly from Paris and Gluck followed the trend. He first composed *La Fausse Esclave*, then *Le Monde renversée* and followed these with five more operas composed in this genre over the next two years. Count Durazzo, the Theatre Intendant and a great admirer of Gluck, encouraged him to write ballet scores, one of which was *Don Juan*.

The stage was now set for Gluck's greatest opera. Count Durazzo introduced him to the librettist of *Orfeo ed Euridice*, Ranieri de' Calzabigi. The two worked on the opera throughout 1762 and the beauty and power revealed at its premiere provided a new experience for the Viennese. The view was that Gluck had surpassed himself.

An important consequence of Gluck's espousal of French opéra-comique was a growing popularity of his music in Paris. The score of *Orfeo ed Euridice* was sent to Paris for printing and an invitation to visit was extended. Unfortunately the Paris Opéra burned down and it was March 1764 before Gluck arrived, accompanied by Count Durazzo.

Gluck was also in demand in Italy and he agreed to visit Bologna in 1763 to compose an opera. His traveling companion was Ditters von Dittersdorff, a young musician whom he had first met as a 13-year-old in Prince Joseph Freidrich's orchestra and who would later be part of the glorious informal string quartet whose other members included Mozart and Haydn. While in Bologna Gluck visited the celebrated old castrato Farinelli. The opera, *Clelia*, was a disappointment.

When he returned to Vienna Gluck experienced another triumph with a new opéra-comique entitled *La Rencontre*. Next, and unusually, he composed music for Metastasio's *Ezio* for which he had already written a full score. Music for the coronation of Emperor Joseph was commissioned, and composed in April 1764. More music was needed for the Emperor's marriage to Maria Josepha the following January, when extraordinarily a number of the women and children of the Imperial family took part in the performance of Gluck's operetta *Il Parnaso Confuso* which was also directed by the Emperor Joseph's brother Leopold. Other works for the occasion, the opera *Telemaco* and the ballet *Sémiramis* were deemed to have subject matter inappropriate for such a happy occasion.

The Emperor Francis died in August 1765 and all the theatres closed for the period of mourning. Then the performance of Gluck's *Alceste* was delayed by the unexpected death of the Empress Maria Josepha. *Alceste* was eventually premiered in Vienna in December 1767 and was so popular that it had two runs of sixty performances each. When the score was published Gluck dedicated it to Archduke Leopold who, as Duke of Tuscany, had invited him to Florence the previous year to conduct an opera called *Ifegenia en Aulide*. In the dedication to this opera Gluck makes one of the most important statements in the development of opera, clearly setting out his philosophy and taking it in a new direction.

By 1769 Gluck was recharging his batteries after years of high productivity. Music for the wedding of the Archduchess Maria Amelia in Parma was produced largely by recycling earlier music. On his return to Vienna the 18-year-old Antonio Salieri was introduced to him and thereafter considered himself a pupil. Generally an astute businessman Gluck invested a substantial sum in a business partnership with Count Afflisio, who managed several theatres in the city. Unfortunately the Count was a gambler who went bankrupt a month later, losing for Gluck a large part of his – and his wife's – fortune.

Gluck started working on his own interpretation of *Ifigenia en Aulide* and negotiated for its performance in Paris. Le Blanc du Roullet, an aristocratic Frenchman who worked at the French Embassy in Vienna, collaborated with Gluck on all the French operas that were to come, and in this case adapted Racine's text himself.

Gluck knew his opera would be controversial and arrived in Paris in November 1773 with his wife and his 13-year-old niece Nanette who now lived with them. Parisian society loved cliques and the German Gluck was up against French traditionalists for whom Rameau was God, and an Italian faction who praised Piccini. Gluck was also soon at war with du Roullet, who refused to change Racine's original text as Gluck wanted, as well as the French orchestra and the singers! The French style was not to Gluck's taste – the French thought it exceptional of course. Unhappy with progress, Gluck postponed the dress rehearsal, due to be attended by the Court, with the result that the King and Queen had to change their schedule for the composer!

In this general conflict with some of the Parisian musical establishment Gluck's cause was supported by the Dauphine, Marie-Antoinette, and her friends. The premiere of *Iphigénie en Aulide* took place in April 1774 and was a triumph for Gluck although the reaction was inevitably mixed. Indeed Jean-Jacques Rousseau stunned his circle by his support for Gluck's work and he wrote the composer a touching letter.

Gluck had been staying with a Duke Christian who suggested that Gluck had the score bound so that he could present it to the king. The Duke and Gluck took a carriage out to Versailles where the composer was presented to Louis XV. Afterwards they returned to the Duke's home and over lunch with friends Gluck was unusually reticent. When taken to task by the Duke he responded: *"I was told that his Majesty rarely spoke to those presented to him. I ought therefore to be pleased to see him stop and talk to me and receive my gift. However, if I write another opera for Paris I would rather dedicate it to a tax farmer, because he would give me money rather than compliments."* Within a month the king was dead.

That summer was spent in Paris preparing the French version of *Orfeo ed Euridice* which was premiered in August and dedicated to Marie-Antoinette, now Queen. Soon Gluck had Voltaire on his side, *"It seems to me that you Parisians are about to witness a great and peaceful revolution in both your government and your music. Louis XVI and Gluck will found a new French nation."* Rousseau's comment was *"If one experiences two hours of such great pleasure, I can understand that life may be worth living."*

Gluck briefly considered living permanently in Paris but returned to Vienna in mid-October. He was confirmed as Court Composer by the new Empress, Maria Theresa, who also gave him permission to return to Paris. She asked that the Paris Opéra might pay a visit to Vienna but this was deemed impossible. *Cythère assiegée* was premiered in Paris in August 1775 but Gluck, his health now giving increasing cause for concern, was too ill to attend.

Alceste was premiered in April 1776 in the presence of Queen Marie-Antoinette. The third act was considered weak and Gluck quickly revised it. Then he received the tragic news that his niece Nanette had died of smallpox in Vienna. Just 18, with a lovely singing voice, intelligence and a warm personality, she was mourned by many, including the Imperial family.

There was an attempt in Paris to produce a secret competition by commissioning both Gluck and his Italian rival Piccini to compose music to the same opera but, in spite of having already commenced work, Gluck burned his score when he heard of this plot. In May 1777 he returned to Paris to compose *Armide* for Queen Marie-Antoinette whom he visited regularly. The choice of libretto was controversial since the revered French composer Lully had set the same work nearly a century earlier. *Armide* was premiered in September 1777.

Gluck returned to Vienna in March 1778 ready to write *Iphigénie en Tauride* and *Echo et Narcisse*, both with French librettists. Unbeknown to him Piccini had again been approached to write on the same subjects. Gluck visited Paris for what was to be the last time in November 1778. *Iphigénie en Tauride* opened in May 1779 and received the best reception of all Gluck's operas. The dedication was again to Queen Marie-Antoinette.

Six weeks later Gluck had a stroke and the premiere of *Echo* was delayed. He made a good recovery but the performance of *Echo* was a flop. Profoundly depressed, Gluck returned to Vienna in October, having assured Marie-Antoinette that he would return to settle in Paris. Determined to prove the quality of *Echo* Gluck sought to produce a version for Vienna. Returning to Paris with its vicious factions held little appeal for him. But the Viennese performance of *Echo*, given in August 1780, was no more successful than the Paris version.

The death of the Empress Maria Theresa three months later was a sad event for Gluck and it caused him to postpone a planned trip to Italy to write more operas. A second stroke the following year made writing impossible but his position was still prominent – he had several operas produced that autumn, much to the disgust of the young Mozart, recently arrived in Vienna from Salzburg. Gluck met Mozart and offered the young composer encouragement. *Alceste* was given successfully in honour of the visiting Grand Duke Paul Petrovitch, the future Tsar of Russia. After the performance the Grand Duke insisted on meeting Gluck.

Gluck's last years were ones of poor health and fame, with many people, notable and otherwise, wanting to visit the master. His wife, as always, looked after him with great care and affection and he continued to have a quiet life in Vienna. An opera that he had put aside,

Les Danaïdes was performed in Paris under his name in 1785, although the music was actually composed by Salieri.

On the afternoon of November 14, 1787, Gluck went for a ride in his carriage with his wife and suffered another stroke. He was taken home but suffered two further strokes that night. At nine o'clock in the morning of November 15 Marianne Gluck summoned Salieri and the two were present when Gluck died at 7 p.m.

Gluck was buried on November 17 in the cemetery at Matzleinsdorf, and afterwards Salieri directed a performance of Gluck's *De Profundis*. The gravestone includes the words *"Here rests an honest German. A zealous Christian. A faithful husband. Christoph Ritter Gluck. Great master of the sublime art of music."*

Gluck *The person*

We have an excellent description of Gluck from the artist Johann Christian von Mennlich, who was Gluck's neighbour in Paris.

> *"Gluck was of above average height, without being stout he was stocky, strong and very muscular, his head was round, his face broad, ruddy and pock-marked, his eyes were rather small and deep-set, but sparkling, fiery and expressive.*
>
> *His nature was blunt, animated and quick tempered. He was incapable of conforming to the rules and conventions of polite behaviour in the fashionable world. Bluntly spoken, he called a spade a spade, and for this reason he would shock the ears of the Parisians twenty times a day. Untouched by praise when it issued from those whom he did not esteem, he only wanted to please true connoisseurs.*
>
> *He was given to copious eating and drinking, without ever becoming intoxicated or dyspeptic. He was self-seeking, unashamedly fond of money, and did not conceal a strong tendency to egotism, especially at table where the choicest morsels belonged to him by right.*
>
> *He never spoke ill, even of his antagonists, but he was at the same time very sparing of praise."*

Gluck was worldly, had good business sense, knew his own worth and mentally was as sharp as a razor. He was a strong leader, disciplined, a perfectionist, demanding. He was indifferent towards his own music once written.

He never worked in the afternoons, his routine was to get up late, to work in the morning, take lunch, go visiting, take supper, then work again late into the night.

Gluck *His Music*

Gluck was arguably the greatest composer living between 1756, when Handel died, and whatever year one gives to the arrival of the genius of Mozart. What is extraordinary is that he is almost forgotten today. But his original position is real. Mozart's debt to Gluck can be seen in his operas. He was an inspiration to Hector Berlioz and an innovator who brought opera half-way to the realism that Mozart was to achieve with *The Marriage of Figaro*. I commend you to join the inevitable recognition and resurrection of the music of Christof Willibald Gluck – there is plenty of it.

To help understand Gluck's impact on opera, excerpts from his dedication to *Alceste* are helpful.

> *"I decided to strip it completely of all the abuses, introduced either by the ignorant vanity of singers or by composers over-eager to oblige, abuses which have for so long disfigured Italian opera, and turned the most sumptuous and beautiful of all spectacles into the most ridiculous and the most tedious.*
>
> *I thought to restrict music to its true function of helping poetry to be expressive and to repeat the situations of the plots, without interrupting the action or cooling its impetus with useless or unwanted ornaments... I also considered that my greatest efforts should be concentrated on seeking a beautiful simplicity.*
>
> *I have avoided making a show of complexities at the expense of clarity: and I did not think it useful to invent novelties that were not*

*genuinely required to express the situations and the emotions. There is
no convention that I have not renounced in favour of the total effect....*

These are my principles."

Remember too the state of opera around 1760. It was more formal
and static, with frequent choruses and dances. Audiences were required
not to be impatient of time but to respond to beautiful music as the
drama unfolded.

The best introduction to Gluck's operas is *Orfeo ed Euridice,* an opera
in three acts which tells the tale of Orpheus and his rescue of his wife
Euridice from the dead. Cupid agrees to her return provided Orpheus
neither looks at her as the couple emerge from the Underworld, nor
Orpheus tells her of the pact. Of course she protests at his apparent
indifference to her and he succumbs. Luckily Cupid is in a generous
mood and Euridice is allowed to return to the world above.

The orchestra is a full one with woodwind, horns, trumpets and
trombones plus harp and chalumbeau. *Orfeo ed Euridice* opens with an
Overture of great rhythmic vitality. *Act 1* is mournful at first, in *Act 2*
Orpheus descends into the Underworld to the accompaniment of
dramatic choruses and dances. Orpheus succeeds in appeasing the Furies
with the beautiful aria *Deh placateri con me* sung against great cries of *No!*
from the chorus. The well-known music in the second scene in the
Elysian fields, *Ché puro ciel (How bright the heavens)* is pure bliss and gloriously orchestrated, flutes fluttering, strings caressing, and a marvellous
oboe counter-melody. The chorus as Euridice is brought to her husband
is deeply moving. The heart of the opera is the ascent out of the
Underworld. Gluck increases the tension to lead us into one of the most
famous arias in all opera, *Ché farò senza Euridice (What is life without
Euridice)* with its glorious melody and profound emotional content. Few
can fail to be moved. After Cupid's happy intervention the opera ends
with celebrations, dances and a final swinging chorus that is not easily
forgotten.

The two *Iphigénie* operas are closely related and are centred on the
Trojan War and Euripedes' tragedy. Both *Iphigénie en Aulide* and *Iphigénie
en Tauride* are tragédie-opéras and both benefit from superbly dramatic
libretti – they are gripping tales.

In *Iphigénie en Aulide* (Aulis is the country) the Goddess Diana demands the sacrifice of Agamemnon's daughter, Iphigenia, who is in love with Achilles. The Greek king protests violently at first but plans to have his daughter killed at the marriage altar. In a blazing row Achilles confronts Agamemnon, but Iphigenia is prepared to accept her fate. The tension builds towards the moment of sacrifice, where there are two different endings. In one Iphigenia is rescued by Diana and taken away to Scythia, in the other Diana intervenes and although Iphigenia marries Achilles he immediately sets sail for Troy.

There's nothing like a brilliant overture to draw the listener into a masterpiece and so it is with *Iphigénie en Aulide*. Its sombre and quiet opening soon gives way to powerful, dramatic, soaring music. The music reflects the unfolding tragedy, with the choruses playing a major role. Listen to the plaintive oboe in Agamemnon's heartbreaking aria *Peuvent-ils ordonner qu'un pére (Can they command a father)*. The appearance of Iphigenia is exquisite, the chorus growing from nothing, and *Act 1* ends with the ravishing love duet between Iphigenia and Achilles.

The first half of *Act 2* is a showpiece. It opens with a graceful chorus, followed by marches, dances and a celebratory chorus for Achilles and the Thessalonians. In the second half the seriousness of the situation is disclosed through the prominent mourning oboe in Clytemnestra's *Par un pére cruel á la mort condamnée (Condemned to death by a cruel father)*. This is followed by the powerful trio of daughter, mother and Achilles, the superb theatrical confrontation between Agamemnon and Achilles, and Agamemnon's later anguished soliloquy.

Act 3 is extraordinarily dramatic and gripping. Iphigenia's acceptance of her fate and her farewell to Achilles are written with great poignancy and emotion. From Achilles' magnificent fiery response to save her, through Clytemnestra's determination to be sacrificed instead of her daughter, the opera rushes to its climax – the sacrifice – only for Diana to arrive in celestial music bringing merciful relief to all. The mood is similar to the conclusion of Beethoven's *Fidelio*. The opera concludes with the obligatory dances for the French Opéra and a martial chorus that add little.

Iphigénie en Tauride takes place after the Trojan War in Tauris, in Scythia on the Crimean peninsula. The barbaric king Thoas rules over a kingdom where every foreigner who lands in his country is sacrificed.

Iphigenia is a priestess whom Thoas approaches because his life is threatened. He wants the sacrifice of two shipwrecked sailors who have been washed ashore. One is actually Iphegenia's brother Orestes, but when he meets his sister he hides his identity, telling her how Clytemnestra, their mother, has murdered their father Agamemnon before being herself killed by Orestes. Orestes is dead, so he says, and the only family member still alive is the sister of Orestes and Iphigenia, Elektra.

Iphegenia resolves to save this sailor by sending him to Elektra in Greece for help, but it is the other sailor, Pylades, who eventually goes. Iphegenia whose function requires that she now sacrifice Orestes, discovers his true identity in time. In a dramatic finale Thoas bursts in and tries to kill both of them but Pylades arrives with help and kills Thoas and the goddess Diana intervenes in the fight between the Scythians and the Greeks. The outcome is that Iphegenia must return to Greece, while Orestes becomes king of Mycenae.

In *Iphegénie en Tauride* Gluck completed his development of opera structure by introducing orchestral recitatives, thus creating a faster moving and more dramatic effect. The *Overture* again begins calmly then generates a storm in which Iphegenie and the priestesses pray. There is a glorious cadence to each verse. The orchestral accompaniment in Iphegenia's sad *"Ô toi qui prolongeas mes jours"* is especially lovely. The Scythian chorus adds a fierce oriental flavour.

Act 2 is high drama opening with baritone (Orestes) and tenor arias in contrast, fiery and tender in turn. Orestes ensuing recitative *"Dieux protecteurs"* and aria are exceptional, the latter almost pianissimo. *"Ô malheureuse Iphegénie"* is ravishing, the oboe ethereally accompanying the mezzo-soprano voice. *Act 3* again provides special opportunities for Orestes and Pylades, individually and in duet. Pylades' delicious aria *"Divinité des grandes âmes"* (*Deity of great souls*) closes the act. In *Act 4* we experience the brilliance of Iphegenia's opening aria with its sparkling string accompaniment, Iphegenia's recognition of Orestes, and the three choruses of Scythians, Greeks and priestesses who finally join together in a lilting and happy conclusion.

Alceste, the opera whose premiere had been postponed by the death of the Emperor Franz Joseph, again involves human sacrifice. Alceste is married to the dying King Admetus who asks the gods to spare him. Not without a sacrifice is their response and Alceste is the required sacrifice. Admetus recovers not knowing that his wife has to die and when he finds out he accuses her of abandoning him. He determines that he will die with her. As the people prepare for this double suicide Hercules, a friend of Admetus, arrives, and declares that he will persuade the gods to relent. As she dies Admetus realises the extent of Alceste's love for him. Fortunately Hercules keeps his promise and brings her back from the Underworld. The opera ends with Apollo's immortalisation of Hercules.

Gluck provides arguably his greatest music for *Alceste*. The opera has an urgent and rich *Overture* leading into several heartfelt choral outpourings accompanied by fanfares. The aria for Alceste *"Grands Dieux"* with its pizzicato accompaniment is Gluck at his superb best and is followed by a double chorus that features throughout the rest of the act. After the first of a number of brief pantomimes for solo orchestra the High Priest, an important part, leads the chorus in passages of exalted music. His call to the Oracle is profound, the Oracle being a model for the Commendatore in Mozart's later opera *Don Giovanni*. After Alceste's acceptance of her sacrifice, another dramatic aria with rich, deep, string accompaniment, *Act 1* ends with a grand scene with the High Priest and Alceste's defiant aria *"Divinités du Styx"*

Act 2 opens with the people rejoicing; there is much happiness in the memorable music until the marvellous third scene when Admetus realises something is amiss. There are a number of glorious arias for Alceste, including a great scene of marital love in *"Je n'ai jamais cheri la vie que pour te prouver mon amour"* (I never loved life but to love you) with its caressing woodwind accompaniment. Gluck shows his mastery of the climax in the last scene. First there is a chorus *"Tant de graces, tant de beauté"* which builds from solo voices. Then Alceste's stunning aria *"Ah, malgré moi, mon faible coeur partage"* (My gentle heart partakes of all our griefs.) is sorrowful at first before it erupts into passionate anger.

In contrast to *Act 2*, *Act 3* opens with the people in a state of grief. Soon Alceste is in despair at the gates of hell to a memorable orchestral accompaniment, *"Ah divinités implacables"*. Admetus arrives ready to die with her and more great love music follows, ending with a duet before Charon, God of Death, calls them – his menace shown through the prominent horn parts. But the rescue by Hercules is dramatic, and the conclusion truly joyful with the chorus in lilting flow.

Ballets

Gluck's ballet music is, as might be suspected, a delight. *Don Juan*, composed in 1761, is for its time extraordinary in its range of expression and was a significant influence on contemporary composers. There are over 30 numbers, almost all short, a succession of pleasures with great variety of dance style, mood, tempo and orchestration. The music biographer H.C.Robbins Landon rightly calls the music "*Beautiful, indeed exquisite*". The concluding number, marking Don Juan's descent into hell, is altogether more serious, dark and dramatic, "*without any question father of the "Sturm und Drang" movement.*"

Gluck's ballet *Semiramis* is just 20 minutes long. Its *Overture*, like parts of *Don Juan*, was to see later re-use in the operas. If one has to choose any one section it would be the magnificent first *maestoso* – just over a minute of magic!

3

WEBER

Weber *His Life*

*C*arl Maria von Weber was born on November 16, 1786, in the provincial town of Eutin, close to Lübeck and the Baltic Sea in the north-western corner of Germany. Carl Maria was the only son of Franz Anton von Weber and his second – and much younger – wife, Genovefa. Franz Anton was over fifty when his son was born and had already fathered eight children in his previous marriage.

A considerable character and a passionate musician, Franz Anton was the brother of Fridolin Weber whose daughter Constanze had married Mozart in 1782. Mozart was therefore Carl Maria's cousin-in-law. In 1758 Franz Anton had held, as a result of his first marriage, an important position in the court of the Elector of Cologne. He had boldly inserted "von" into his name, assuming a title of nobility to which he had no right. This was very much in his character. But now, as a mere town musician Franz Anton's career was on the wain.

Carl Maria was a sickly baby, born with a defect in his right hip that was to cause him to limp throughout his life. Soon he was leading a peripatetic life as his father decided to form the Weber Theatre Company. This troupe included many of Franz Anton's extended and musical family and was soon permanently on the road giving performances throughout southern Germany. The young Weber therefore lived a bohemian life with his education coming from his family rather than schools. Music and painting were his main interests at first and when the touring was interrupted by his mother's poor health Carl Maria was able to benefit from receiving piano lessons from a young musician, Johann Heuschkel.

When his family settled in Salzburg for a time Franz Anton sent his 11-year-old son, for whom he had great ambitions, to be trained by Michael Haydn, brother of the famous Franz Joseph Haydn. Weber

Carl Maria von Weber

studied composition and wrote some piano pieces but at the end of 1798, after the death of Genofeva von Weber from tuberculosis, the Weber troupe moved on to Munich where music lessons resumed under new teachers. Weber's first opera was the main fruit of this period but the score, along with other early compositions, perished when a fire destroyed the cabinet in which it was stored. Weber, who had inherited a superstitious nature from his mother, took this as a bad omen.

Weber's father had chosen Aloys Senefelder as a publisher for his son. Senefelder was at this time perfecting the new process of lithography, a means of reproducing drawings, and Weber worked as Senefelder's assistant. Soon it looked as though father and son might use the knowledge they were gaining about printing to their commercial advantage. Luckily for music, Weber's interest waned and he composed another opera *Das Waldmädchen*. The new opera was premiered in Freiberg in November 1800 and later reached Vienna.

A year later the Webers returned to Salzburg and the professional relationship with Michael Haydn resumed. A third opera *Peter Schmoll* was written and given its premiere in Augsburg in 1803 by Weber's brother Edmund, conductor of the local theatre orchestra. A move to Vienna followed, with an introduction to Franz Joseph Haydn, but the great composer was now too old for teaching. Instead Weber turned to the Abbé Georg Vogler, a larger-than-life character with a reputation for demanding hard work from his pupils.

The delightful Viennese experience was cut short by Weber's audacious appointment – on the recommendation of Vogler – as Kapellmeister of Breslau at the tender age of 17. Inevitably his youth created difficulties and jealousies and his new-found delight in the opposite sex and a string of love affairs caused further complications. Weber was a serious and innovative conductor, changing the layout of the orchestra to advantage and weeding out poor singers and trivial (but often commercial) operas.

An appalling accident almost halted Weber's burgeoning career. Busily composing in his study he reached out for a flask of wine, not knowing that his father had filled it with acid for engraving. He swallowed some of the highly corrosive liquid and passed out in agony. Luckily a friend came by and Weber was rushed to a doctor. His life was saved but his attractive singing voice was ruined and it took two months for him to be able to resume work. Weber's critics had taken full advantage of his absence to undermine his position and, disgusted at his treatment, he resigned. His lifestyle had also created a significant number of creditors who, on hearing of his resignation, clamoured for payment. It was necessary to move on.

One of Weber's pupils who was a maid of honour to the Duchess of Württemburg effected an introduction that led to Weber being offered the position of Intendant in Duke Eugen's court. He accepted and arrived with his father and an aunt in tow. Life on the idyllic ducal estate at Carlsruhe in Upper Silesia was exactly the tonic that Weber needed and although his position was unpaid, all his practical needs were taken care of and he dined at the Duke's table. He was also safe from Napoleon's encroaching armies. Amongst his compositions were two symphonies dedicated to the Duke.

It is unclear why Weber moved on but, armed with the offer of a position in nearby Stuttgart as private secretary to the Duke's brother Ludwig, Weber left in February 1807. It was five months before he arrived, after taking time to visit friends and give concerts. He found himself in a totally unsuited role in a dissolute court. Ludwig, his patron, was the younger brother of Friedrich, who had the title of King of Württemburg. This enormously overweight and homosexual king took a dislike to Weber and even had him imprisoned for insubordination on one occasion. Nonetheless Weber's two years in thriving Stuttgart were productive. He composed prolifically – the opera *Silvana* dates from this period – and mixed in a wide artistic circle in which the composers Spohr and Danzi were prominent, the latter becoming a good friend.

Weber's time in Stuttgart ended dramatically and acrimoniously soon after his 75-year-old father arrived from Carlsruhe, double bass strapped on top of his carriage, to join with his son. Weber had been given money by Duke Eugen for the purchase of horses and Franz Anton appropriated it to pay off his own debts – he was that sort of person! In order to retrieve the situation Weber had to resort to a moneylender who had an eye for future favours.

The money-lender, a local publican, finding Weber could not help to exempt his son from conscription into the army, petitioned the king for the return of the loan. The king took the opportunity to have Weber arrested. The police arrived at the theatre while *Silvana* was in rehearsal and took Weber away to be locked up in solitary confinement. After 16 days the king decided to free him to avoid embarrassing disclosures but Weber's creditors had him rearrested. Weber negotiated a repayment schedule and, with his father, was deported with almost nothing in their pockets apart from some letters of introduction from Danzi.

The letters led them to Mannheim where Weber was able to place his father in accommodation. Then, unencumbered, he moved a short distance down the Rhine to Darmstadt where his former teacher Abbé Vogler and an old friend, Johann Gänsbacher, now lived. He also met Vogler's latest pupil, Jakob Beer, soon to become famous under the name of Giacomo Meyerbeer. Weber agreed to the publication of several of his works by the publisher Simrock, although at this time he was spending as much time earning money by writing about music as by performing and composing.

Weber first met his future wife, a soprano called Caroline Brandt, whilst on a concert tour with Vogler, and in September 1810 she sang in the premiere of his latest opera *Silvana* at the tender age of 16. The *Piano Concerto No. 1* was completed in the following month and another opera *Abu Hassan* soon followed. By dedicating the opera to the Grand Duke Ludwig, Vogler's patron, Weber was able to earn some sorely needed funds. However, he was unhappy about the way his career was developing and he decided to embark on a concert tour.

Soon he was in Munich with introductions to the court. Most importantly Weber developed a close friendship with one of the most celebrated clarinettists of the time, Heinrich Bärmann. The virtuoso asked Weber to compose a piece for him and the resulting *Concertino for clarinet and orchestra* was premiered before the Queen of Bavaria in April 1811 and greeted with rapture. So impressed was the King that he immediately commissioned two full concertos for the instrument.

Weber's star was at last in its ascendancy and *Abu Hassan* was premiered two months later, quickly followed by the clarinet concertos. After the premiere of *Clarinet Concerto No. 2* Weber bid farewell to Munich and set off on a concert tour with Bärmann. Their travels took them to Prague, Dresden, Leipzig and Weimar (where Goethe attended one of his private concerts) and on to Berlin where Weber conducted his opera *Silvana* with great success. During his time there he stayed with Jakob Beer's parents and also found himself in a fascinating

33

intellectual and artistic circle. Sad news arrived that his father had died at the ripe old age of 78.

Weber accepted an invitation to revisit the Duke of Saxe-Gotha and whilst there composed his *Piano Concerto No.2*. Needing to earn money to pay off his father's debts he next set off, via Leipzig, to Prague, arriving in January 1813. Almost immediately his fame brought him the offer of directing the Prague Opera under very attractive terms and he quickly accepted, seeing himself at last able to pay off his creditors. Sorting out the opera house was to be a major challenge. To lead the orchestra he engaged Franz Clement, the dedicatee of Beethoven's *Violin Concerto*, and amongst the new singers hired was Caroline Brandt, who had written to ask him for a position.

Weber was very susceptible to attractive women and started a liaison with one of his singers, Therese Brunetti. Married and with a string of lovers, Therese led Weber a merry dance until he realised the very different and superior qualities of Caroline, who lived a quiet life with her mother. She, however, got cold feet on several occasions at the prospect of marrying Weber and it wasn't until the end of 1816 that they officially became engaged, after many lovers' tiffs. One of the major works Weber composed during this period was a cantata *Kampf und Sieg*, written to celebrate the defeat of Napoleon at Waterloo in June 1815, another was the *Clarinet Quintet*, composed for Bärmann.

Prague bade farewell to Weber with great regret in October 1816 and by the end of that year he had been offered the position of Kapellmeister of the German Opera at Dresden, the court of the King of Saxony. The new appointment had its problems as the Court was extraordinarily formal and dull and there was a rival Italian Opera that was considered much more fashionable.

When Weber discovered that Morlacchi at the Italian Opera had a higher rank he handed in his resignation, and would withdraw it only when he was given equal status with Morlacchi. He was keen to create truly German operas and he persuaded the poet Friedrich Kind to write a libretto based on the tale of *Der Freischütz*, which had long appealed to the composer. The libretto rights were acquired and Weber set to work on the score, inevitably suffering many distractions.

The work for the Dresden Court became increasingly onerous and it was November 1817 before Weber was able to get away to Prague to marry Caroline. Their honeymoon took the form of a concert tour of song recitals throughout Germany so that the couple could build up funds before returning to Dresden for Christmas. A condition of the marriage had been Weber's insistence that Caroline give up her stage career.

Weber's innovations didn't make his life as Kapellmeister easy – he conducted with a baton instead of from the fortepiano and again tried to alter the orchestral layout. He also, remarkably, had problems in having his own works performed. Domestic life was much happier at first, in spite of Caroline's continual jealousy. She gave birth to a daughter in December 1818 but the health of the whole family was fragile and the baby died at three months. Weber's health had been poor from childhood and he was now suffering from tuberculosis. The death of the baby, combined with his inability to perform his compositions, left him profoundly depressed for a period.

Gradually recovering, he completed the score of *Der Freischütz* and incidental music for a play, *Preciosa*. He quickly moved on to another opera, *Die Drei Pintos*, (which remained incomplete until Gustav Mahler finished it many years later, using other Weber music). Caroline lost another baby in 1820 and soon afterwards the couple set off on another concert tour during which a further pregnancy occurred. Caroline was left in Hamburg whilst her husband continued on to Copenhagen where he was given a warm welcome and the *Overture* to *Der Freischütz* had its premiere. With Caroline he returned to Dresden, another miscarriage occurring on the journey.

May 1821 saw the Webers in Berlin for rehearsals of *Der Freischütz* which was in competition with Spontini's *Olympie*. Weber, by encouraging the creation of magical effects, exploited the supernatural elements of his opera, which was *"received with the most incredible enthusiasm"* as he noted in his diary. Soon after the premiere he gave a performance of his brilliant new *Concertstück für Piano* and the enthusiasm for his music in Berlin contrasted dramatically with the indifference with which he was received when he returned to Dresden in July. Nonetheless Weber liked living in Dresden and, not for the first time, turned down an extremely attractive alternative opportunity.

Der Freischütz was quickly taken up by many of the opera houses in Europe, and the impresario Domenico Barbaja gave Weber another commission for Vienna. Unfortunately Weber had fallen out with his librettist, Friedrich Kind, who felt inadequately recognised after the success of *Der Freischütz*, and he had to look elsewhere for a librettist. For the tale of *Euryanthe*, a medieval romance and a difficult dramatic subject, Weber settled on Helmina von Chezy who although a talented writer was inexperienced in opera.

Weber had at last been given permission to stage *Der Freischütz* in Dresden but was still disappointed when his request to stage *Die Drei Pintos* was turned down. Determined to ensure *Der Freischütz* was a success Weber was meticulous in preparing the opera and was at last rewarded by the rapture of his local audience. Amongst the thousands who heard *Der Freischütz* was the nine-year-old Richard Wagner on whom the music and drama had a profound influence. Wagner's step-father (or possibly father) Ludwig Geyer sang under Weber on numerous occasions. Afterwards Weber left for Vienna to discuss *Euryanthe*, and met Schubert and Salieri amongst others. In April Caroline at last gave birth to a healthy boy, Max Maria, much to the parents' delight. But Weber's health continued to deteriorate and he did not expect to live long.

The libretto of *Euryanthe* gave Weber many headaches because of the limitations of Helmina von Chezy but he completed the score in the summer of 1822 and started rehearsals in Vienna, where Rossini's operas were currently popular, with his usual thoroughness. Earlier he had produced Beethoven's *Fidelio* and entered into a correspondence with the master. Beethoven was aware of Weber's new opera and Weber visited the great man who promptly took him out to lunch and promised to try to attend the premiere.

Vienna has always been notorious for its gossip, and rumours soon spread of the poor quality of the story of *Euryanthe*. Helmina also started to cause problems, ultimately making a scene at the premiere by arriving at the last minute and shouting *"make way for the poetess"* as she was lifted over the audience's heads to her seat. The opera was deemed a success although its length caused many in the audience to leave before the end. Beethoven was not present but Schubert was, and was very rude about the opera. It was withdrawn after 20 performances.

On Weber's journey back to Dresden he conducted the 50th performance of *Der Freischütz* in Prague and arrived home ready to stage *Euryanthe* by royal command. His health was still deteriorating – he was now seriously ill – and he had no energy for composing. Weber's doctor was very blunt and told him that he needed a year's complete rest or he could be dead within weeks.

Euryanthe was acclaimed when it opened and, while Weber's attempts to have the opera performed in Berlin were thwarted, invitations from Paris and London opened up new possibilities. In August 1824 the impresario Charles Kemble of the Covent Garden Theatre in London offered the commission of a new opera and, fatefully, Weber's desperate desire to provide for his family led him to accept. It was particularly galling for him that at the same time *Der Freischütz* was achieving great success in Paris under the title *Robin des bois* with a libretto by the French writer and critic Castil-Blaze and without any payment of royalties to the composer. Pirated versions were also heard in London.

The composition of *Oberon* was commenced in February 1825, shortly after the birth of another son, Alexander. Weber took his forthcoming visit to London very seriously and took English lessons to make himself fluent. In the summer he visited Weimar (and was kept waiting for another meeting with Goethe) before resting in the spa of Ems. Weber arrived incognito, but once the town discovered his identity he was feted everywhere. *Euryanthe* was finally performed in Berlin in December with Weber conducting, it was acclaimed at the premiere but survived for only a handful of performances.

Weber had a premonition that he was not going to return from London. His philosophical view was "*Whether I stay or whether I go, in one year I will be dead anyway. But if I go, my children will have bread when their father dies; if I remain, they will starve*". Weber set off via Epernay and Paris, where he spent five days. He called unannounced on Rossini, who was appalled at his wasted appearance, and was visited by Cherubini. Berlioz sought him out unsuccessfully.

Weber set out from Paris on March 2, 1826, and arrived in London three days later, having had a seizure near Calais. An express coach with four horses took him to London to be met by Sir George Smart, with whom he stayed, treated like royalty. Weber's initial concert at Covent Garden was rapturously received – the applause was deafening and prolonged.

Most of Weber's energy went into preparing *Oberon* and despite some major difficulties with the soloists (not unusual!), the opera was premiered on April 12. He had an overwhelming ovation both before and after the opera. He conducted twelve more performances of *Oberon* over the next few weeks and then prepared for a benefit concert. But throughout this exhausting period his strength was ebbing away, he was coughing up blood, and he was in despair at not being with Caroline, to whom his letters hid his true condition. By the end of his last concert, poorly attended because of competing attractions and a major horse-racing event, he was close to death.

Weber's thoughts were now focused on a speedy return to Dresden and his wife and children. His departure from London was set for June 6, but it was not to be. He spent much time exhausted in bed but still got up for musical events. Moscheles, the famous pianist whom Weber had known for many years, visited twice. After a couple of glasses of port with Smart, Weber retired to bed in Great Portland Street on the evening of June 4 and died during the night behind the locked door of his bedroom. The door had to be broken open in the morning and Weber's body was discovered. The official cause of death was given as consumption. Weber had prepared meticulously for his death, and his affairs were well organised and documented.

Weber's body was embalmed and the funeral was held in St.Mary's, Moorfields, on June 21, 1826. In the intervening days a benefit concert had been held for Weber's family. The hearse was drawn by six black horses. The church was filled with musicians and friends and the coffin was carried into a vault to the *Dead March* from Handel's *Saul*.

Some 15 years later the inappropriateness of Weber's resting place was recognised in Germany and pressure built up to return his remains to Dresden. Richard Wagner, now also Kapellmeister at Dresden, repaid his indebtedness to Weber by organising the event. Max Maria von Weber, the composer's elder son, was studying in London and arranged the exhumation.

Weber's coffin arrived in Hamburg in October 1844 before being loaded onto a boat for the last stage up the River Elbe. Freezing weather delayed the arrival of Weber's body but on December 14 a torchlight procession awaited the coffin, with eighty wind instruments and twenty muffled drums playing music from *Euryanthe*, arranged by Wagner. The next day Weber was laid to rest in the Friedrichstadt cemetery. Wagner delivered a profound and moving oration – a unique tribute from one musical genius to another.

Weber *The person*

Weber was short, slim, with a faintly red tinge to his brown hair. He had blue-grey eyes, narrow shoulders and a long thin neck under a long face and nose. He had large hands with very long thin fingers, wore spectacles and walked with a very pronounced limp. He suffered from delicate health and a nervous disposition, and was prone to moods and depression. He had more than a touch of naivety and was not the strongest of characters. He liked the good life in his bachelor days.

He was generous, honest, had integrity (once when he performed a Meyerbeer opera he returned a consequent gift of silver candlesticks to the composer's parents), was loyal and had many friends. His marriage was a happy one and he took delight in his children.

He was highly intelligent and had a wide set of interests that could detract from his composing, although *"Perseverance leads to the goal"* was his motto. Weber was a great supporter of things German in music and somewhat intolerant of foreign influences. He had a considerable facility with languages and was an excellent guitarist as well as a brilliant pianist.

Weber's innovative thinking led him to be a creative conductor who also paid great attention to detail in order to achieve the best effects – he was in advance of his time in wanting to control planning, casting, production, lighting, costumes, and scenery in addition to conducting. His career as a kapellmeister limited the time he was able to devote to composition but he was also hampered by his lack of self-confidence and ability to persevere. He suffered from – and found it difficult to combat – the political intrigue common in music circles.

Weber *His Music*

Weber had a melodic gift given to few composers (to say that he is in the same league as Mozart and Schubert is not far-fetched) and his greatest themes have achieved universal popularity, even if the composer's name is less known. One of the earliest truly romantic composers, the originality of his opera *Der Freischütz* had a profound influence on other composers in the early 19th century, particularly Wagner and Berlioz.

It is the genius shown in Weber's greatest works that justifies an exploration of those that are less well-known. Patience can unearth gems, particularly when played by gifted performers who believe in Weber's genius.

The "Weber Starter Pack" contains some stunning works:

1 Overtures There is no better introduction to Weber than the music that introduces his operas - it would be amazing if you weren't bowled over by the glorious melodies of the overtures to *Euryanthe, Oberon, Der Freischütz* and his earlier operas. Sweeping melodies abound and there are great orchestral climaxes as well as intimate and delicate music. Clearly there is a genius at work. If you aren't in love with Weber's music after listening to the magnificent Hanover Band recording, then I'll be amazed!

2 Clarinet Quintet Weber's relationship with Heinrich Bärmann inspired several great works for clarinet amongst which the four movement *Quintet* is particularly masterly. Its *allegro* opens with mellow strings ushering in a perky melody on the clarinet. Urgency contrasts with serenity. The *fantasia*, beautiful and intimate, is a rhapsody with nostalgia never far away, the richness of the cello matching the clarinet. The *menuetto* justifies its *capriccio presto* marking and is deliciously playful except in the Schubertian *trio*. The concluding *rondo* is a joyful affair, galloping along and ending with a stunning virtuoso passage for the clarinettist.

3 Concertino for Horn This is a delectable little work exuding happiness in a brief passage. A showcase for the soloist, it has an extraordinary passage two thirds of the way through where the horn, after descending to its lowest notes, has to play whole chords – a first for the instrument. After this innovation the concertino concludes with a gorgeously memorable melody, with a lilting and martial gait – exquisite! A must-hear ending!

4 Der Freischütz is one of the great romantic operas, filled with a magnificent variety of numbers – for male chorus, female chorus, arias, duets and trios. Set in the Bohemian countryside, it is a tale of the occult. The hero Max is a hunter who can succeed to the position of head forester (and marry the present incumbent's daughter Agatha) only through a supreme test of marksmanship. Unfortunately his aim has deserted him and a fellow huntsman, Kaspar (in league with the devil, Samiel) persuades him to use magic bullets that always find their target. The two repair to the Wolf's Glen, a desolate and eerie place, where the bullets are cast during a growing storm. Kaspar knows that one of the bullets is destined to kill Agatha, but when Max fires the shot a wise hermit intervenes and it is Kaspar who is hit and killed. Max is given a light sentence, he has to serve just a year's probation for his sins, after which Agatha and the head forester's post will be his.

Weber's music is gloriously rich, and matched to a good libretto the result is overwhelming. Choruses and hunting horns abound (the horns have a field day in the last act), as do great themes. In *Act 2* Agatha's lovely aria, memorably trailed in the *Overture*, leads into a charming duet with her cousin. The following trio with Max surely provided inspiration for the love music in *Act 2* of Wagner's *Tristan and Isolde*. After the stunningly evocative music for the *Wolf's Glen Scene* (its eerie effects caused a sensation when first heard), the lilting folksong for the bridesmaids in *Act 3* is in supreme contrast. The conclusion is exultant.

Concertos

The concertos written for the clarinet and piano offer great music and give much pleasure. *Clarinet Concerto No.1* opens stealthily before a swinging and majestic theme for the orchestra takes over. The stealth returns with the entry of the clarinet then the mood alternates between happiness and nostalgia, intimacy and declamation. The clarinet leads the *adagio* in an exquisite hymn-like song of beauty and tenderness. Half-way through there is a sublime transition as solo horns enter and blend with the clarinet. You may know the first theme of the concluding *rondo*, with its joyful hunting call.

Clarinet Concerto No.2 has a very different mood, more classical than romantic. It opens dramatically with full orchestra leading to an elegant second theme. The clarinet enters as if to tell a story – an exciting one!

The *andante* is almost Mozartean, and there is a rollicking virtuoso finale, *alla polacca*.

In the same league is the *Concertino* which has a *Theme and Variations* sandwiched between an *adagio* and a *finale*. *Don Giovanni*-like chords open this delightful work whose theme is full of possibilities, graceful, jolly, ruminative, rhapsodic, mysterious. Towards the end we are dancing in a fast waltz-time before the brilliant conclusion.

Piano Concerto No. 1 is a virtuoso work, with a strong romantic vein in its classical structure. The first movement has weight and lyricism in equal measure. The *adagio* is an absolute gem, the piano accompanied by two solo cellos, with violas, double bass and horns in a mood of mellow intimacy. The final movement is an exciting *presto* with a thrilling conclusion.

Piano Concerto No. 2 opens with a powerful rush then melts into a feminine second theme. The entry of the piano states clearly that this is a virtuoso work, the piano passages are dazzling at times. The tender *adagio* is highly original, producing a quiet but radiant effect created by the muted and divided strings. The concluding *rondo*, unusually rich and varied, is a dramatic show-stopper.

The Konzerstück in F minor opens in introspective mood, with dominant piano. Suddenly it becomes very agitated and draws in the orchestra. The piano has some magnificent passages before quietness descends. A march introduces the jubilant *finale* – a very hummable tune, opening gently and building to a majestic declamation that unleashes Weber's virtuosity in a thrilling conclusion, the soloist drilling down the keyboard.

For further exploration there is the *Bassoon Concerto*.

Symphonies

Weber's two early symphonies also give much pleasure and have no ambition to profundity. The opening *allegro con fuoco* of *Symphony No. 1* has a second theme of great beauty and perkiness that contrasts with the dramatic and fast-moving opening. Weber develops his inventive ideas towards an exciting conclusion. You cannot but be entranced by the beguiling *andante* with its prominent woodwind. The tremolando effect of the strings is a precursor to the music of the Wolf's Glen scene in *Der*

Freischütz. After the classical *scherzo* the *presto* uses horns and woodwind as principal operatic voices in a bustling and brilliant conclusion.

Symphony No.2 opens like a *sinfonia concertante*, the oboe and bassoon gentle foils to an orchestra that beats out its assertive rhythm before the horn enters. This joyful movement – longer than those to follow – develops much momentum. The *adagio* is ravishing, highly original, horns introducing a solo viola, then oboe in a mood of great intimacy. Later the full strings sing out a simple version of the initial theme – glorious! A brief *minuet*, with a delicate *trio* led by the oboe, is followed by the concluding *scherzo presto*, also brief – and with a joke ending which I leave you to discover!

Piano Music

Weber's piano music is sadly neglected but contains much that is beautiful and virtuosic. Weber wrote his piano music for his own performance and as he had large hands that could span an octave and a half, some of his music is extraordinarily difficult for many pianists.

He wrote four sonatas of which the greatest is *Piano Sonata No.2*. Inevitably it opens with a memorable melody, starting a rich and romantic journey. Quiet, hesitant notes introduce the *andante* but it flowers into an ardent romance, mainly in march-time. The *menuetto capriccioso* is brilliant in its effects, the much slower middle section has a lovely theme of great simplicity in the right hand, leaving brilliance to the left hand. The *rondo* opens with another theme that you won't forget, languidly running in different directions before returning home. This sonata is Weber at his best, another concert hall showstopper, although this time with a quiet ending.

Piano Sonata No.1 has an opening *allegro* – playful and imposing by turn – and a singing *adagio* – ravishing in the right hand – with a theme very similar to that in the last movement of *Sonata No.2*. The brilliant *menuetto* is longer and more serious than usual and has a highly original *trio* with contrasting feminine and masculine elements. The concluding *rondo* is a *perpetuum mobile*, a pianistic tour-de-force that concludes an appealing and original work.

The first movement of *Piano Sonata No.3* has the unusual marking of *allegro feroce* and is appropriately powerful, but with a lyrical second theme. The singing *andante con moto* is lovely in its simplicity and the concluding third movement, *allegro di bravura*, brilliantly integrates three themes.

Piano Sonata No. 4 takes more time to appreciate. It has a much more serious mood than its predecesors, in spite of a Mozartean episode in the opening movement. The *menuetto* comes second, marked *presto*. The *andante quasi allegretto* is marked *consolante*, not that it seems appropriate to this restless movement. The concluding *La Tarantella* is the closest to lightness that this sonata achieves.

The *Invitation to the Dance* makes its fullest impact in the ravishing orchestration by Berlioz but it is good to hear it in its original form, and the comparison is fascinating. It is a highly original and beautiful work in waltz-time, the theme totally memorable and appropriately languid, exuding joy. Weber provided an intriguing story line.

The *Polacca brillante "L'Hilarité"* is short, great fun, melodic and highly rhythmic, an ideal virtuoso work. Weber also wrote numerous sets of variations of which *Seven Variations on Bianchi's air "Vien quà, Dorina bella"* is gorgeous, romantic and melodic. *Seven Variations on an Original Theme (J.55)* is another delight.

Chamber Music

The *Grand Duo Concertante* brings together the clarinet and piano, both instruments for which Weber writes brilliantly. A work of beauty and virtuosity, it opens with an *allegro con fuoco* where the instruments spark off each other, like a young couple getting to know each other and delighting in each other's conversation. In the *andante* the clarinet opens with a sustained melancholic theme before the assertive piano briefly takes over. The concluding *rondo* is brilliant, the high spot a dramatic passage where the clarinet sings to the accompaniment of piano tremolos. The ending will bring the house down.

Operas

Weber's mature operas are grossly neglected, unknown to many opera lovers. Not only are they works with glorious melodies, great drama, arias and choruses, but they are also a source of much of Wagner's inspiration.

Euryanthe has exceptional music and the reputation of the libretto's weakness is somewhat exaggerated. Euryanthe of Savoy is pledged to Adolar, Count of Nevers in the reign of Louis VI of France. Adolar's enemy is the jealous Lysiart, who challenges him to a wager on Euryanthe's constancy with their respective lands at stake. Eglantine, Euryanthe's enemy, worms a secret from her while she is away from the Court of Nevers. Lysiart and his knights arrive at Nevers at the end of *Act 1*, and in *Act 2* Lysiart inevitably teams up with Eglantine before escorting Euryanthe to the Court. His knowledge of the secret wins him Adolar's lands. In *Act 3* Adolar and Euryanthe are cast out and because of his feeling of betrayal he plans to kill her. When a serpent appears she tells him to flee while she acts as a decoy but Adolar kills the serpent and then abandons her. She is saved by the King's hunt and when she tells the full story, the King promises full restitution. In the concluding scenes Adolar discovers the true story just as Lysiart is about to marry Eglantine in Adolar's castle. Adolar intervenes and Lysiart and Eglantine are denounced. (She is killed by her co-conspirator). Euryanthe recovers from a broken heart and the lovers are reunited.

The *Overture* gets the opera off to a fizzing start and leads into the lovely opening chorus of the knights and ladies, the first of many pageant choruses that are one of the glories of the opera. The *cavatina* for *Euryanthe* is an exquisite pearl, similar in style to that in *Der Freischütz*. Weber gives Eglantine superb declamatory music after her early triumph, then trumpets lead into the chorus as Lysiart arrives. *Act 1* ends with Euryanthe and chorus in lilting partnership.

Act 2 opens with high drama and Lysiart's demanding show-piece of treachery and vengeance. Later the duet with Eglantine has great power, and the contrast with the opening of the subsequent intimate love aria for Adolar, another high-spot, could hardly be greater. His following love duet with Euryanthe is truly rapturous. The tension of the final scene is palpable, the music of the highest quality, the characters utterly true, the concluding section displays Euryanthe's desolation and the powerful vindictive denunciation of the chorus.

In *Act 3* the serpent scene concludes with another of Weber's glorious *cavatinas* for his heroines before another mark of his genius, as his multiple horns announce the rousing *Huntsmen's chorus*. Euryanthe's duet with the King marks the turning point of the opera, she then breaks into a joyful and soaring aria, with the following chorus O

Jammer, unerhört! (O grief beyond compare) showing great sensitivity. Weber recycles one of his best tunes for the opening aria of the last scene. The choice of instruments for the wedding march of Lysiart and Eglantine produces a touch of the grotesque, and then events rush to the conclusion in which Euryanthe and Adolar's duet leads into the final exultant chorus.

Oberon is a magical opera in more ways than one. Like Mozart's *The Magic Flute* in numerous ways (it could justifiably be called the *Magic Horn!*) it suffers from spoken passages, unfashionable today. It would be my third choice Weber opera.

Oberon is the Elfin king who has fallen out with Tatiana over the issue of whether men or women are more dependable in love. They have vowed to remain apart until one or other of them has found a truly faithful couple. As a penance the knight Huon of Bordeaux has been given an impossible errand; he is to go to Baghdad to abduct and marry the Caliph's daughter Rezia. Oberon's servant Puck ensures that Huon and Rezia have visions of each other to assist the process of falling in love. Oberon gives Huon a magic horn for protection and the fairies provide a magic passage to Baghdad. In *Act 2* Rezia is due to marry a local prince but Huon intervenes, kills the prince and with the help of the magic horn escapes with Rezia, her friend Fatima and his squire Sherasmin (who of course also fall for each other). Oberon creates a number of trials, the first a shipwreck from which they are all sold into slavery. In *Act 3* they find themselves in the palace of the Emir of Tunis. Rezia is in the harem and Huon and Rezia are sentenced to death. But Oberon's horn saves them, and Oberon and Tatiana transport the two pairs of lovers magically back to the Court of Charlemagne and great celebrations.

Oberon's horn opens the *Overture* in a mood of mystery before introducing one of the famous themes of the opera. The music soon opens out into a scintillating orchestral introduction to the opera. The opening chorus is for whispering fairies, setting the magical tone. Shortly afterwards the chorus is in full voice. In Huon's first main aria the cello repeats the glorious theme contained in the overture. The concluding scene of *Act 1* between Rezia and Fatima has a memorable duet and chorus.

Act 2 opens with a distinctive Turkish flavour and majestic music. Later Puck's invocation of the spirits is thrilling, concluding with the storm. Rezia's *Ocean! Thou mighty monster!* is one of the most famous of all opera arias. After the words *And now the sun bursts forth* the trumpet theme rises and accelerates towards the outburst and introduction of the great melody. The *finale* of *Act 2* is a merry and magical interlude for Puck, Oberon and their friends.

The highlights of *Act 3* are Rezia's *Cavatina*, Huon's *Rondo* and the swinging chorus that succeeds it. The *Finale* has splendour, fanfares, great melodies and a rousing choral conclusion.

Gustav Mahler was able to complete the mature work *Die drei Pintos* by appropriating other music by Weber, and this would be the next opera to explore if you enjoy those above. After that lie the earlier *Silvana* and *Abu Hassan*.

Other Music

Weber wrote a wide range of other music including cantatas, masses and songs that are largely forgotten or rarely performed. The delights that we know suggest there is a lot more buried treasure.

R. Schumann

48

4

SCHUMANN

Schumann *His Life*

Robert Alexander Schumann was born on June 8, 1810, in Zwickau, a small town in Saxony. He was the youngest of five children, three sons and two daughters, born to August Schumann, a successful bookseller, author and publisher, and his wife Johanne. The family was thus reasonably well off even during the economic and political crises created by the Napoleonic Wars. When Robert was three his mother contracted typhus and he spent the next few years with friends, the Ruppius family.

At the age of six the young Robert started at a private school. A year later he had his first piano lessons with the church organist and before long he was making his first efforts at composing. He came to develop a gift of improvising and creating musical portraits. The young Schumann progressed quickly and was particularly inspired when he sat in front of the famous pianist, Ignaz Moscheles, at a concert.

August Schumann supported his son's interest by ensuring that piano tuition continued and that there was a good piano at home. In Zwickau Schumann would often make music with friends such as the Carus family or with his piano teacher. Music was not Schumann's only interest however; he was blessed with intelligence and imagination and was an avid reader. He became an ardent fan of the romantic writer Johann Richter, known as Jean Paul, and would write poems that emulated the florid style of his idol. As Schumann discovered girls at an early age his writing provided a useful outlet for his emotions.

The Schumann household might have seemed to be happy and straightforward on the surface but the parents had underlying tensions and neuroses and, it can be seen with hind-sight, some hereditary problems. In 1826 when Schumann was sixteen his 29-year-old sister Emily committed suicide and his father died in August of the same year . Both were severe blows and Schumann was distraught. As a consequence of

August Schumann's death Schumann inherited a reasonable sum of money, although the capital was held in trust, with the income payable on condition that he went to university.

Two years later Schumann left Zwickau to attend the University of Leipzig, ostensibly to study law. He boarded with a relative who helped to introduce him to university life, which was very different from Zwickau. One of the closest friendships he made was with Gisbert Rosen, another Jean Paul enthusiast and the two set off on a tour together during one of their first University vacations. They visited Jean Paul's widow in Bayreuth and also the poet Heinrich Heine in Munich.

On his return to Leipzig Schumann was delighted to find that Agnes Carus, whom he had often accompanied on the piano at her uncle's house in Zwickau, had moved to Leipzig with her husband. Schumann, who was a little in love with Agnes, was able to renew his music-making with her. Amongst new acquaintances was the piano teacher Friedrich Wieck from whom Schumann started to take lessons. Wieck had a nine-year-old daughter Clara whom he was training as a piano virtuoso and Schumann got to know this precocious child who was to become his wife twelve years later. At this time law was the furthest subject from Schumann's mind, the piano the closest, and writing not far behind.

The death of Franz Schubert in 1828 at the age of just 31 was a great sadness for Schumann – he sobbed throughout the night after he heard the news. Schumann revered the little known Schubert above all other composers and was much influenced by him. Although his lessons with Wieck were developing Schumann's technique and his early compositions showed promise, he was not happy in Leipzig.

Schumann decided to move for a year to Heidelberg University where his friend Rosen was studying. There he found a music-loving professor, Anton Thibaut, who was able to arouse in Schumann some enthusiasm for law. Thus life in Heidelberg was much more convivial and Schumann took particular pleasure in attending Thibaut's weekly soirées where guests were expected to sing choral masterpieces. By now Schumann was an excellent pianist and this made him welcome in Heidelberg society. He also experienced more frequent auditory disturbances. *"Terrible, half the night with eternal sounds. Buzzing and poetry in my ears"* read a diary entry.

Schumann heard the great violinist Paganini in April 1830 and was inevitably bowled over. The pleasurable student life in Heidelberg continued but by the summer Thibaut had persuaded him to give up law and Schumann prepared to go back to Leipzig to study with Wieck. He needed his mother's support to follow a career in music and he asked her to get in touch with Wieck who would be able to convince her of her son's talents. Wieck replied positively but - knowing Schumann well - with the proviso that it was essential that the budding composer/pianist applied himself.

Schumann found that he had much leeway to make up – probably Clara, now eleven, was a better pianist. He went to live with Wieck and it was soon apparent that the pupil/teacher relationship was not going to be easy - Wieck was a strict disciplinarian and unsympathetic to Schumann's self-indulgent nature (he was a heavy drinker and smoker by this time and was often chasing women).

Schumann also started composition lessons with Heinrich Dorn, the music director at the theatre. The *Abegg Variations*, which he considered to be his first mature work, were published in 1831. For a period Schumann considered becoming a pupil of Hummel in Weimar and moving there with his mother, but nothing came of it. He was also writing a novel!

In 1831 Schumann created two imaginary characters, Florestan and Eusebius, an idea that stemmed from Jean Paul. He was to use them for dialogues about life and music. He also developed an intimate relationship with a girl called Christel, almost certainly a member of the Wieck household. In May of that year Schumann acquired a newly published score by the unknown Frederic Chopin and was immediately bowled over by it. He started a career as a music critic when his review of Chopin was eventually published in the leading German music journal, the *Allgemeine musikalische Zeitung*. The famous words "*Hats off, gentlemen, a genius*" put Chopin's name on the musical map of Europe.

When the Wiecks set off on an extended concert tour for Clara and his lessons and lodgings ceased, Schumann became profoundly depressed and almost suicidal. A problem with the middle finger of his right hand, first experienced in 1830, resurfaced under the stress. However he pulled through and composed *Papillons*. A performance in Zwickau, where Schumann stayed for much of 1832, of the first movement of a symphony was a disaster, whereas Clara's *Scherzo for Orchestra* was applauded.

Unfortunately when Schumann returned to Leipzig in March 1833 and started composing piano pieces in earnest, he contracted malaria. It was after this that the relationship with Clara Wieck became a romantic one. But a profound depression and breakdown was just around the corner. It was probably triggered by the death of Schumann's brother Julius at the age of 28, from tuberculosis in August, followed by the death of his beloved sister-in-law, Rosalie, from malaria in October. Schumann was again close to suicide. It was Schumann's close male friends who pulled him round, particularly Ludwig Schunke, a fellow musician of the same age who came to live with him. Schumann created the Davidsbündler, a semi-real, semi-fantasy, group of progressive artists, headed by the fictional Florestan.

With Wieck, Schunke and a piano teacher, Julius Knorr, Schumann founded a progressive music magazine *Neue Leipziger Zeitschrift für Musik* which first appeared in April 1834. Schumann became editor and quickly dominated the magazine with a unique style, often using the Davidsbündler, and Eusebius and Florestan, for contrasting perspectives. His partners were largely sleeping ones and Schunke died at the end of 1834 from tuberculosis

Any ambition to be a virtuoso pianist had evaporated by now. Schumann's problem finger was now paralysed. The causes of this ailment, a disaster for someone with ambitions to be a brilliant pianist, are unknown, but range from excessive use of a mechanical device to strengthen his finger discipline to early symptoms of the syphilis which was eventually to drive him insane and kill him. In spite of taking numerous remedies, including putting his hand in the entrails of a newly slaughtered animal, the malady did not improve and Schumann was forced to concentrate on composition.

Clara was sent off to Dresden for further tuition by her father and in her absence Schumann fell in love with another of Wieck's pupils, Ernestine von Fricken, and the couple became secretly engaged in 1834. Schumann had second thoughts when he found out that she was illegitimate and dropped her in the autumn of 1835. Schumann was left with the idea of composing some piano pieces using the musical notation of ASCH, the name of Ernestine's home town.

Leipzig had formed an orchestra in the eighteenth century that had taken its name from the Cloth Hall (Gewandhaus) used for its concerts. In 1835 the already famous Felix Mendelssohn, still only 26, was appointed as musical director and the two composers got to know each other well. Chopin was another visitor to Wieck's house, so Schumann was mixing in good musical company.

By now Clara Wieck had reached the age of sixteen and was already known as a brilliant young pianist. The mutual affection between her and Schumann had developed over the years and was now turning into something much deeper. In January 1836 Schumann proposed and her reciprocated love helped him to bear his mother's death in the following month. But if Schumann thought that Wieck would be delighted with the prospect of having him as a son-in-law he was quickly disillusioned. Clara was effectively Wieck's pension fund, his creation in every way as he saw it, and Schumann certainly didn't meet his ambitions for his daughter.

Forbidden to see Clara by Wieck, Schumann suffered another bout of depression and not for the first time he started to drink heavily. Attempts to maintain contact by sending Clara his new compositions were a failure, but his works of that time, including the *Fantasie*, were inspired by his feelings of love for her. For once Schumann persisted and in August 1837 they again committed themselves to marry. On Clara's 18th birthday Schumann formally wrote to Wieck asking for his daughter's hand in marriage but met with no more success than on the previous occasion.

Emotionally on a high, Schumann was highly productive and *Novelletten, Davidsbündlertänze*, and *Kriesleriana* were written at this time. The couple considered moving to Vienna and Schumann undertook an exploratory visit. Whilst there he visited one of Schubert's brothers, Ferdinand, and was astonished to discover a wealth of unpublished works by the prolific genius. Schumann took this great treasure to the leading publishers, Breitkopf and Härtel, but with an eye for a masterpiece he sent Schubert's last symphony directly to Mendelssohn. Thus Schubert's *Great C major Symphony*, whilst difficult to play, was premiered in March 1839 and achieved a resounding success.

Schumann suffered another blow when his brother Eduard died the following month, and back in Leipzig the relationship with Wieck sank ever lower. In the face of Wieck's persistent refusal to agree to the marriage Schumann persuaded Clara to apply to the court for permission to marry. Wieck threw his daughter out of his home and commenced a vicious campaign against Clara and her fiancé. Wieck's totally unreasonable behaviour did not go down well with the court and Clara eventually won her case in July 1840. It would be more than three years before she was reconciled with her father.

During this traumatic period Schubert befriended another great composer/pianist, Franz Liszt, who had arrived in Leipzig. Schumann dedicated his *Fantasie* to Liszt, a kindred romantic spirit. It was a period of great inspiration and Schumann composed his two great song cycles, *Liederkreis* and *Dichterliebe*. Clara and Schumann were finally married the day before Clara's 21st birthday, on September 12, 1840.

Married life was marvellous but had the difficulties inevitable between two artists living together. Clara needed to tour as a concert pianist to earn money, her husband needed peace and solitude to compose. His *Symphony No. 1*, called the *Spring*, was premiered by Mendelssohn and the Gewandhaus Orchestra in March 1841 and coolly received. In September Clara gave birth to the first of a succession of children, a daughter Marie, further complicating the family situation. Further children were to arrive at approximately two-year intervals throughout their marriage. Another symphony, in D minor, was completed but withdrawn after its premiere.

The Schumanns toured together in 1842, Clara's piano-playing proving more popular than Schumann's compositions. On their return Schumann turned his attention to chamber music, writing three string quartets and following them with a piano quartet and quintet. Appointed a professor at Leipzig's Music School the following year he was also visited by the French composer, Hector Berlioz.

Clara and her husband embarked on a longer tour in 1844, eventually reaching St. Petersburg and Moscow. During the trip Schumann's mental health deteriorated, perhaps induced by the stress of travel. On his return he resigned as editor of the *Neue Leipziger Zeitschrift* and started ineffectively on several opera projects. By the autumn he was in a bad state and started to have hallucinations.

At the end of the year the couple decided to leave Leipzig and move to Dresden. Schumann's health improved somewhat in the new surroundings. The music director at the opera was Richard Wagner but when the two composers met they didn't take to each other, Schumann preferring the company of the more refined Mendelssohn with whom he collaborated in arranging the publication of the complete works of Johann Sebastian Bach. The *Piano Concerto* was finally completed and given a private premiere by Clara and the Dresden orchestra in December 1845 and Schumann completed another symphony, published as his second the following year.

In spite of now having four children the Schumanns set off for Vienna at the end of 1846 to give a series of concerts which had only a limited success. After their return Schumann started to write an opera *Genoveva* and was appointed Director of the Dresden Men's Choir. However, he lacked the necessary self-confidence to be a good conductor and it was undoubtedly a stressful role.

The Schumanns lost their next child and were also deeply upset by the death of Mendelssohn in November 1848. Following the spate of revolutions in Europe triggered by the French revolt against the monarchy in 1848, there was an uprising in Dresden in May 1849. Wagner was deeply involved and was forced to flee as, briefly, did Schumann and his wife, leaving their children behind before Clara returned to rescue them. The trauma – the revolution was brutally put down – jolted Schumann into a period of prolific composition which saw the creation of the *Concertstück for Four Horns and Orchestra* and the *Rhenish Symphony* amongst other works.

Genoveva was eventually premiered in June 1850 but did not please the Leipzig audiences. Life in Dresden had returned to normal but Schumann was not happy there. It was suggested that he apply for the position of Music Director at Düsseldorf and when his application was successful the Schumann family moved once again. Schumann was initially well received and was able to conduct many of his own works. But criticism of his conducting began to build up so that by the end of 1852, with his health noticeably deteriorating, he had lost the confidence of the orchestra and singers. Schumann's symptoms became increasingly worrying, his memory and speech increasingly impaired and he suffered spells when he became irrational. He also developed a strong interest and belief in the supernatural.

In May 1853 Schumann revised his early *D minor Symphony* and it was premiered at the Lower Rhine Festival. There he heard the young violinist Joseph Joachim and was inspired to write the *Violin Concerto* for him. It was through Joachim that a young composer visited the Schumanns in September. It was the 20-year-old Johannes Brahms, complete with compositions, and the Schumanns recognised his outstanding talent immediately. Thus commenced a close artistic and personal relationship.

By the end of 1853 Schumann was suffering more frequent periods of mental instability and he was clearly unfit to conduct. By February of the following year he was losing his sanity, hearing music playing in his head. On the 26th Schumann tried to persuade Clara to have him committed to an asylum but his doctor ordered him to stay in bed at home. Schumann, wearing only a coat, bolted from the house into a stormy night and threw himself into the River Rhine. Rescued by nearby fishermen he was returned to his home.

This experience proved the point he had been trying to make and within a few days he was taken to a private asylum at Endenich near Bonn. Clara, on the doctor's advice, was not allowed to visit her husband, even though he had periods of rationality, so the birth of their last child, Felix, in June was a poignant event. Although they wrote to each other, her dreams of her husband's recovery were dashed towards the end of the following year when she was told that he would never recover. Almost certainly it was syphilis that was the cause of his gradual destruction, although there were periods of remission.

By the summer of 1856 the end seemed near. Clara visited Endenich for the first time on July 14 and returned for the third and last time with Brahms on July 27. Only then was she allowed to see her husband. Schumann seemed to recognise her. She remained close by him but Robert Schumann died peacefully and alone in his sleep in the afternoon of July 29. Clara had gone to the railway station to meet Joachim and was told the news on her return. She visited his room half an hour after his death and laid flowers on his brow. Later she wrote *"I stood by the body of my beloved husband and I was at peace. All my feelings were taken up in thanks to God that Robert was at last free."*

The simple funeral was held two days later in Bonn, with Joachim and Brahms the principal mourners as Clara bade farewell to her husband.

Schumann was buried that evening in the cemetery near the Sternentor in Bonn. Thirty-nine years later Brahms saw Clara buried beside her husband.

Schumann *The person*

Schumann was of medium height with long, slightly wavy, hair and a handsome appearance. He was intelligent and very much of a romantic disposition, a dreamer and intellectually curious. He was almost as much a poet as a composer.

He was indulgent before his marriage, often irresponsible, weak and overwrought. He spent money easily, and smoked and drank too much. He was moody and prone to depression and loss of self-confidence. But he was loyal and developed some deep friendships. He was diligent enough to keep a detailed diary for most of his life. He was outspoken and honest, usually objective and generous. His sense of the contemporary music that would stand the test of time was unusually perceptive

He could be indecisive and was not a leader. But in matters to do with art, composing or writing he showed application and dedication. Marriage (and Clara's complementary character) gave Schumann a stability and love that he craved and encouraged his sense of responsibility. Theirs was one of the greatest musical marriages, although it had the inevitable stresses that there would be between a great composer and an exceptional performing musician who also raised a large family.

Schumann *His Music*

Schumann was an inspired romantic genius with a consequent musical character that was unlike any other. He frequently rejected classical formats in favour of his own structures, where expression and melodic invention were paramount. If some of the works do not entirely succeed that is hardly surprising in a passionate risk-taker, and one who eventually lost his reason.

There are some delectable works in the "Schumann Starter Pack":

1 Carnaval is described as *Scènes mignonnes sur quatre notes (ASCH)* and the variations have titles such as *Eusebius*, *Florestan*, *Chopin* and *Paganini*. It is a tour-de-force, a thrilling work with memorable melodies that builds steadily to a conclusion that is truly stunning, an almost unbelievable cascade of notes as the theme returns majestically and then accelerates away.

2 Symphony No.4 After a pregnant opening this D minor work generates a rushing and rhythmic theme with enormous momentum. Tension is created by strong trombones, the rhythms becoming fiercer until the orchestra explodes and enters the major key. The short *romanza* opens with melancholy woodwind over a trudging pizzicato before the cellos lead in the strings. Later a solo violin comes down in a benediction. Fiery rhythms open the *scherzo* whose *trio* meanders on a descending scale, awaiting the repeat when it provides the bridge to the *finale*, reminiscent of the similar passage in Beethoven's *Fifth Symphony*. Mystery descends and a quiet theme on the violins, tremolo strings and trombones explodes into the major key. The orchestra sets off in exultation, destined for a thrilling conclusion.

3 Piano Concerto The composer's best known work, it is in almost every concert pianist's repertoire. Orchestral chords punctuate the soloist's entrance statement before the first great theme, melancholic, whimsical and catchy, is introduced. Next we are off on a restless theme of great momentum and noble potential. Schumann creates a dramatic and totally gripping movement with these two contrasts, expressing every range of emotion from sadness to nobility. A brief *intermezzo* concludes with notes that erupt into the concluding *allegro vivace* and a bouncy theme. The ending is barn-storming.

Symphonies

Schumann's symphonies are a great pleasure, the greatest being the five-movement *No.3, Rhenish*. The opening of this consistently inspired work has enormous swagger, sweep and energy on the way to its exultant climax. The *scherzo* is a superb representation of the River Rhine, flowing and eddying with a broad swinging theme. It is followed by a tribute to Cologne Cathedral. A dramatic brass chorale opens the majestic slow movement, the heart of the work. The concluding movement is one of Schumann's jolly affairs, some might say not quite appropriate to what has gone before. If it is a little weak thematically Schumann's conclusion is a tour-de-force, where a marvellous melody is led by the horns before the chorale returns in triumph.

Symphony No. 1, Spring is a much under-estimated work. It opens with magnificent fanfares that die away into a passage for solo flute that leads to an orchestral explosion and a bustling theme full of momentum. Reflective passages where woodwind dominate provide a counterbalance, but you are swept along to a thrilling ending with rushing violins and returning fanfares. The slow movement opens with a glorious yearning Schubertian theme on the violins. The cellos, bathed by balmy woodwind, take us onward – the music is beautiful, the mood rapt. Trombones bring this gem of a movement to a close. A heavily accented and rustic *scherzo* follows, then, after a flourish, the *finale* sets off with a frolicking light-weight theme – it provides a marvellous foil for the stately and noble theme that follows. Schumann keeps you on the edge of your seat as he builds tension and teases you until the symphony sweeps home in thrilling style, horns, trombones and trumpets to the fore.

Symphony No. 2 is an elusive work that needs a great interpreter to show its full qualities. It opens with a brooding *adagio* but eventually an outburst of brass leads into a pulsating *allegro*, woodwind and strings inciting each other to a climax. The movement is episodic, the quality of the themes less than the energy, bustle and fierce rhythms, but there is an exciting conclusion. A bustling *scherzo* is great fun, brilliantly orchestrated and again leading to a great climax. The beautiful *adagio* is marked *espressivo*, the theme of the pulsing strings is taken up by the oboe and bassoons. Much use is made of wind instruments to provide interludes between singing string passages. The concluding *allegro molto vivace* again has a strong rhythmic opening – the orchestra is in full flood and when it has the principal theme the effect is overwhelming. There is a bit of padding but the climax, with trumpets again to the fore, is worth waiting for.

Concertos

The *Konzertstück for four horns and orchestra* is an exhilarating masterpiece, a veritable tour-de-force for the glorious French horn. It is a virtuosic piece, all the horns having formidable parts, the themes memorable throughout, whether lyrical, noble or fanfare-like. The slow movement opening is deeply reminiscent of Weber at first, then displays quiet grandeur. Trumpets announce a joyful *finale* that has some stunning sonorities before an inevitably rousing conclusion.

The beautiful and neglected *Cello Concerto* has a rhapsodic opening movement with the soloist dominating. Schumann's themes recur throughout the concerto and the transitions between movements are seamless. The short slow movement is a gem, beautiful and pensive, with some truly glorious harmonies from the cello. The concluding rondo is joyful, with strong rhythms as so often with Schumann.

The *Violin Concerto* was withheld from publication until the 1930s as the manuscript was owned by the Joachim family. It has a beautiful and full orchestral introduction before the violin arrives on the scene. The solo part seems more a commentary than a lyrical lead, but the orchestration is rich and symphonic and the lower strings regularly add powerful momentum. The slow movement, the heart of the work, is a lovely outpouring, and it leads straight into a happy finale where Schumann again leaves the main melodies with the orchestra. The concluding chorale is particularly memorable.

The *Fantasia for Violin and Orchestra* is Schumann at his most lyrical, immediately displayed in its surging opening. The work has an introduction, main part, cadenza and a brief epilogue. The violin is given the themes in this work, but the climax is the orchestral introduction to the cadenza. The brilliant ending is another chorale.

Orchestral

The *Overture, Scherzo and Finale* is essentially a short symphony lacking a slow movement. In this work the spirit of Mendelssohn is never far away. The *Overture* is light and graceful, the *Scherzo* has the same rhythm as that of Beethoven's *Ninth Symphony* – but in more playful mood. The *Finale* is formidable, displaying typical Schumann energy and rhythm with woodwind choirs over strings. It builds to a triumphant chorale with the return of the main theme to create a magnificent ending.

The *Overture Manfred* is a lyrical and dramatic work, soon getting into gear with trumpet fanfares after a slow introduction. The themes are memorable, the tension and momentum significant before a quiet and sombre ending.

Piano Music

Schumann's instrument was the piano and he is most famous for the relatively early works where his *"compressed genius"* created many musical miniatures – miniatures in length, not impact.

The *Symphonic Studies, Opus 13* is a set of 12 variations on an andante theme. They are mostly very brief, Schumann jewels, but ending up with an extended finale. *Etude No.4*'s perky march-like theme surely reappears in Bruckner's great *Fifth Symphony* fugue. It is thrilling to follow the unfolding variety. The penultimate study, *con espressione* is particularly beautiful and leads into a stunning *finale*, a memorable melody that scales the full keyboard.

Kinderszenen, Opus 15 (Scenes from childhood) consists of 13 miniatures, again of about a minute each. Just listen to the opening to discover that they are gorgeous, suffused with simplicity and gentleness. *Träumerie (Dreaming)*, as you would expect, is magical and timeless. The titles of other pieces such as *Catch me* and *Almost too serious*, suggest humour in abundance but Schumann ends in a mood of serenity with *Child falling asleep* and *The Poet speaks*.

Kreisleriana, Opus 16 consists of eight *fantasies* each lasting for about 3 or 4 minutes except for the second which, incorporating two *intermezzi*, is double the length. The *fantasies* are large scale and no titles are given. In the wide variety of tempo and mood, the slow pieces *(sehr langsam)* are particularly beautiful but the fast pieces have a surprising delicacy, particularly the last where Schumann eschews a sensational ending.

Papillons (Butterflies), Opus 2 is a theme and variations, the theme totally gorgeous and memorable, lilting as it rises and falls in the right hand. Each variation lasts around a minute and there is a strong sense of flitting from one to the other, even if some of the butterflies are more like eagles in their sturdiness. The theme returns at regular intervals throughout.

Davidsbündlertänze Opus 6 has 18 dances *(Characteristic pieces)*, more little Schumann gems. With Schumann at his most concise there is no chance of longeurs; melodies pour out one after the other, and quite a few linger in the memory.

Schumann's Fantasie Opus 17 is *"the most passionate thing that I have ever composed – a deep lament for you"* as the composer wrote to Clara. It opens with an urgent lyrical theme with an agitated accompaniment, before a serene second subject takes over. Glorious music flows towards the beautiful quiet ending. The second movement is dominated by a memorable and flamboyant march with a brilliant peroration. The concluding movement is dream-like, a rich out-pouring of lovely melody and a conclusion that rises gradually to a passionate climax before its lingering reflective ending.

The passionate and inspired *Sonata No. 1* was announced as *"Sonata for pianoforte, dedicated to Clara from Florestan and Eusebius"* It has an ardent introduction leading into a fast syncopated melody that gives way to a romantic song-like second subject. The aria that follows *(senza passione, ma espressivo)* is gorgeous, intimate music. The *scherzo ed intermezzo* takes us back to *Carnaval*, an exceptionally rich third movement. The *finale* is a phantasmagorical experience, with themes, ideas and brilliance cascading over the listener.

Sonata No. 2 in F minor opens with an *allegro brillante* of restless power and grand scale. It is the work of a genius in full flow. Next come two scherzo movements, followed by a *quasi variazioni* based on a sad theme of Clara's to which Schumann brings optimism and brilliance. The *prestissimo possibile* is a tour-de-force; the pianist rushes ever faster, the listener is enthralled.

Sonata No. 3 in G minor contains something of Beethoven's force and structure. The opening movement has a fiercely rhythmic main theme, a languid second and great momentum. The *andantino* is like a heart-breaking operatic aria and the following brief *scherzo* catapults us into the *rondo: presto*, which is a scintillating piece with a few essential pauses for breath.

The *ABEGG Variations*, Schumann's *Opus 1*, is a brilliant short piece, the notes of the name creating a memorable rhythm. After the theme come four variations and an extended finale. The *cantabile* final variation is close to, but earlier than, Chopin.

Chamber Music

The *Piano Quintet* is considered by many to be the masterpiece of Schumann's chamber music year of 1842. In four movements, the first is a brilliant affair, the piano leading. Next comes *in modo d'una marcia*, an extraordinary and intimate fantasy movement of great ingenuity. After this somewhat shattering experience – not unrelated to the *scherzo* in Schubert's *String Quintet* – we have a more rational *scherzo* and *finale*, brilliant and exuberant.

Schumann's *Piano Quartet* is a gem of a work, of instant appeal. It's gorgeous opening, slow and rapt, quickly leads into a joyful *allegro ma non troppo*. The return of the opening is highly effective. After a brief scampering *scherzo*, Schumann gives us an *andante cantabile* of beauty and intimacy, in which the cello is initially dominant. Schumann keeps up the inspiration in a *finale* with an exciting fugal conclusion.

Schumann's *String Quartets* have been likened to the *Rasumovsky Quartets* of Beethoven. These related works are amongst the best of the genre after Beethoven and Schubert, and instantly enjoyable in their full romantic glory. *String Quartet No.2* opens with a passionate main theme, constantly evolving; the second movement *andante quasi variazioni* is intense and verging on the spiritual. The *scherzo* is robust, with a delightfully witty cello-led trio, the *finale*, in its bustle, is reminiscent of the conclusion of the *Spring Symphony*.

A slow and passionate falling figure opens the glorious *String Quartet No.3*, leading to a swaying allegro that has some exquisitely intimate passages. Next comes an intriguing movement, an *assai agitato* that turns into a set of variations of brilliance, sensitivity and resolution in turn. The *adagio molto* is an heir to Beethoven, an intense hymn of beautiful simplicity. Schumann concludes with a rich and uplifting *finale* in which one can often imagine a full orchestra.

The opening of *Violin Sonata No.1* is initially dominated, psychologically, by the piano. It is a passionate, lyrical affair. Next comes an *allegretto*, whose mood is initially sad and reflective and later becomes excited. The *finale* is agitated all the way to its striking conclusion.

Violin Sonata No.2 opens in most dramatic form, the violin questing and leading into an energetic and extended movement. Next comes a brilliant *scherzo*, followed by a slow movement of great simplicity and purity at first, manifested by pizzicato violin, which becomes passionate with gorgeous double-stopping, rendering two themes on the violin. The concluding movement is a galloping affair, concluding an enjoyable work.

The *Piano Trios* offer many pleasures for Schumann lovers and not just in the slow movements. In *Piano Trio No.1 in D minor* listen out for the radiant and delicate passage that breaks, halfway through, into the energetic flow of the first movement. A fiery *scherzo* precedes a melancholy slow movement with violin and cello in gorgeous duet. It runs straight into the *finale*, a rich melody and a superb ending.

The lovely *Piano Trio No.2 in F* opens with a leaner sound, the themes memorable, the mood gay. Next comes a lovely singing slow movement, followed by one that is like a delicate intermezzo. The *finale* has a strong staccato element as it bounds along.

Piano Trio No.3 has a gorgeous waltz-like second theme in its opening movement, at whose ending the instruments evaporate away. The slow movement is another violin and cello duet of tranquil beauty, the third movement is reminiscent of the opening of the composer's *Fourth Symphony*, and the conclusion is lilting.

Stage Works

Schumann was another great composer much attracted by Goethe's *Faust*. His *Scenes from Goethe's Faust* is an oratorio, set on a great canvas, and perhaps my favourite work in the genre. Two hours long, it is in three parts, the first concentrating on Gretchen, the second on Faust, the third on transfiguration. The music is Schumann at his most romantic and dramatic as heard immediately in the intense and dark *Overture*. Highlights in *Part 1* are the sensitive music given to Gretchen and the great concluding drama in the cathedral where an Evil Spirit tempts her with the foreboding *Dies Irae* in the background. The mood of the opening of *Part 2* is exquisite pastoral happiness, giving way to nature paintings. At *Midnight* there is an eerie, spectral scherzo with four grey women, Want, Guilt, Worry, Distress, confronting Faust who sings "*Night presses around me, deeper and deeper still. And yet within me beams a radiant light.*" set to most noble music, brass resplendent. Next comes *Faust's Death* and his confrontation with Mephistopheles. The relentless tread gives way to a moving farewell from Faust, a fanfare farewell and soliloquy from Mephistopheles, and a lovely hushed choral ending. Schumann exploits the full potential of Goethe's play in *Faust's Transfiguration*, gorgeous, heavenly music. Listen to *Pater Profundus*, sombre brass giving way to surging strings and ravishing woodwind; noble Angels with great spatial effects, heavenly trebles leading to a thrilling climax. In the home straight, Doctor Marianus brings us ecstatically to the harps and flutes. The final passage *Alles Vergängliche* is restrained at beginning and end, exploding in the middle before quiet trombone chords have the final say.

Das Paradies und die Peri is a secular oratorio like *Scenes from Faust*. The plot concerns a woman (a Peri), born of a fallen angel and a mortal, and her quest to be admitted to paradise. She fails with her first two offerings to Heaven but succeeds with the third, the tears of a criminal moved by a child at prayer. In *Part One* listen to the sublime simplicity of *Wo find'ich sie?*, the thrilling chorus that follows, the wonderful fugal culmination that will surely leave you enthralled. *Part 2* has corresponding beauties, the exquisite *Verslassener Jüngling* for example, which runs through a tingling sequence into a languid finale of sleep. *Part 3* concludes with a noble chorus *O heil'ge Tränen inn'ger Reue (Blessed tears of soul-felt penitence)*, eventually leading into a grand choral celebration, *Willkommen*, that erupts into total exhilaration – truly nearly unknown, but truly magnificent.

Schumann's opera *Genoveva* has been called "*A great symphony with voices*" reflecting the weaknesses of the libretto compared with music that is Schumann at his best. Genoveva is the young bride of Siegfried, Count Palatinate, and is left when he goes off to war against the Moors. His friend Golo is entrusted to look after Genoveva but tries to seduce her instead. Margaretha, Golo's nurse and a witch, plays an important part throughout the opera. Siegfried is led to believe that Genoveva has committed adultery in his absence and tells Golo to kill her. He leaves the task to the servants but Siegfried, now knowing the truth, returns to save Genoveva. The music is certainly masterly, as the *Overture* and the first love duet quickly show. There are many stirring choruses and the action is mainly fast-moving. As expected of a great song-writer the arias, particularly for Genoveva, have great melodies and mood. The conclusion is heart-warming and gently triumphant.

Choral

Requiem for Mignon is a superb setting of a text by Goethe for chorus, orchestra and soloists – particularly boys' voices. It opens with a funeral march but takes an increasingly positive view for the mourners. Schumann's setting is uplifting and beautifully crafted as it moves to its thrilling climax and gentle ending. It surely influenced Brahms.

Nachtlied is a setting for chorus and orchestra, marvellously evocative and delicately written. The first stanza celebrates the night, the second celebrates life, and the third is an invocation to sleep. Thus Schumann creates a slow, fast, slow movement with a great climax in the central section, trumpets chanting, before the lovely approach of sleep. A little gem.

Songs

The full scope of Schumann's genius is demonstrated in his songs, amongst which are some of the most beautiful ever written. Below are some of the song cycles that are justly famous but there are dozens of individual settings of genius from amongst the many songs he composed. As an example of these listen to *Die beiden Grenadiere (the two Grenadiers)*, two soldiers vanquished with Napoleon in Russia, which ends with a gloriously defiant *Marseillaise*.

Start with *Frauenliebe und Leben (Woman's Life and Love)* which is a glorious song cycle to idealistic poems by Albert von Chamisso. The first quiet chords and the entry of the mezzo soprano voice will immediately convince you of the quality of this work After the rapture of *Since I first saw him* we have the joy of *He, the noblest of all*. Schumann's melodies are inspired throughout the eight songs. The rippling piano accompaniment of *Help me, O sisters* is a marvellous foil to the radiant voice. In *Sweet friend, you gaze* the singer lets her husband know she is pregnant in a song that is unbelievably moving. Death comes at the end with *Now you have hurt me for the first time.* Schumann brings back the opening theme, alone on the piano, to conclude a great experience.

Dichterliebe (Poet's love) comprises 16 settings of Heine's poems, a romantic and gentle cycle of considerable depth. Each song lasts just about a minute. Each is a gem, and each depicts a different situation. My favourite for drama is *No. 9 Das ist ein Flötea und geigen (What a piping and fiddling!)* but for beauty it is *No. 12 Am leuchtenden Sommermorgen (This glowing summer morning).* Schumann wraps up the cycle with a profound piano solo.

Liederkreis, Opus 24, a wonderfully intimate set of songs, consists of nine settings of Heine. Listen to the beautiful sotto voce *No. 3,* the spectral *No. 4,* the gorgeous *No. 5* (the heart of the cycle) and the singer's farewell to his lover's hometown. *Song No. 7* and the concluding song *Mit Myrten und Rosen* are equal to their surroundings.

The more famous *Liederkreis, Opus 39* consists of twelve settings by Joseph von Eichendorff. They have a dark nocturnal character which also appears to be in search of optimism. Their riveting power is apparent from the initial gentle *In der Fremde (in the Unknown).* *Forest Discourse* is pregnant with expectation, *Mondnacht (Moonlight night)* is rapt, the melody supreme. *Wehmut (Melancholy)* has a lovely melody, but for originality the mysterious *Zweilicht (Twilight)* wins. *Frülingsnacht (Spring Night)* brings the set to an exuberant end, the piano part brilliant.

Twelve Lieder Opus 35 consists of 12 settings by Kerner. A further collection of little gems, this set consists of twelve songs in which the piano is particularly passionate. *Wanderlied* is amongst the most beautiful but most moods are depicted and captured superbly.

F. Liszt

5

LISZT

Liszt *His Life*

Franz Liszt was born on October 22, 1811, in the small Hungarian town of Raiding, 80 kilometres from Vienna. He was – unusually for the time – the only child of Adam and Anna Maria Liszt. Adam's family had worked on the land in Hungary for several generations and he managed sheep farms for Prince Nicolas Esterházy II, Haydn's patron. Adam Liszt was a highly talented amateur musician, proficient on many instruments. He had played the cello under Haydn and sung in the choir when Beethoven conducted the first performance of his *Mass in C*.

Young Franz grew up in these rural surroundings. He was a delicate child, often sick with fevers, an ailment to which he remained vulnerable throughout his life. He was close to death more than once. Music dominated the household where Adam played the fortepiano and wandering gypsies passed through regularly with their vibrant melodies. The family was religious and, for a brief period in his youth, Adam had gone so far as to join a Franciscan order.

Liszt was taught to read and write by the village schoolmaster who had the task of teaching over 60 children in a small room. Liszt was five-years-old when his father discovered he had a natural talent for music and was attracted to the piano. Adam became his first teacher, and gave his son a good grounding in the works of Bach, Mozart and Beethoven. On his seventh birthday he was given a piano by a business acquaintance of his father and within a year Prince Nicholas heard him play and agreed to provide assistance. The young boy's aptitude was remarkable and at the age of eight he started to write his own compositions.

Adam knew that his son needed better tuition and in 1819 he took his son to Vienna to play for Carl Czerny, Beethoven's former pupil who was the leading piano teacher in the city. Czerny said of the audition: "*He was a pale, sickly-looking child who, while playing, swayed about on the stool as if he were drunk... I was astounded at the talent which nature had bestowed on him."* Czerny advised Adam on how to improve his son's playing and agreed to take him as a pupil when the family moved to Vienna.

Liszt first appeared in public at a concert in a town near Raiding in 1820, playing a concerto and improvising on themes suggested by the audience. He had an even greater success with a second concert of his own in the traditional Hungarian capital, Pressburg, attended by much of the Viennese nobility. As a result six noblemen offered to provide 600 florins for six years to enable Liszt to have the best tuition.

Thus Adam made the courageous decision to give up his secure position in Raiding for his son's advancement and the family moved to Vienna in 1822. Liszt started daily piano lessons with Czerny and the teacher noted: *"Never before had I so eager, talented or industrious a pupil."* Czerny was a hard taskmaster and he forced Liszt to undertake many exercises and to develop his sight-reading even further. Composition was undertaken with almost equal intensity under Salieri, who wrote to Prince Nicholas begging him to give financial support and saying *"I heard young Liszt by chance in a certain house while he was sight-reading and improvising on the piano, he has left me so entranced that I actually believed I had been dreaming."* Neither teacher charged for lessons.

The 11-year-old Liszt was soon well enough known to be one of 50 composers invited to write a variation on a waltz theme by the publisher Diabelli – Beethoven, dismissive of both the theme and the concept, wrote his great masterpiece *"33 Variations on a theme by Diabelli"* as his own response. Liszt made his Viennese debut at the end of 1822 to rave reviews The *Allgemeine Zeitung* reported *"A young virtuoso has, as it were, fallen from the clouds and compels us to the highest admiration. The performance of this boy, for his age, borders on the incredible."*

Adam persuaded Czerny to arrange a meeting with his young son's hero, the reclusive Beethoven, who disliked prodigies. The meeting went well, Liszt ended by playing the piano part of the first movement of *Beethoven's Piano Concerto No.1.* Liszt recounted many years later: *"Beethoven caught hold of me with both hands, kissed me on the forehead and said gently: "Go! You are one of the fortunate ones! For you will give joy and happiness to many other people!"* Liszt said that this occasion was the proudest moment of his life. The virtuoso was later to play a major role in propagating Beethoven's difficult late piano works such as the *Hammerklavier Sonata*.

Liszt left Vienna after giving a final concert in the famous Redoutensaal in April 1823. He hoped that Beethoven would attend but was disappointed. After giving a number of acclaimed recitals in Hungary he set off with his family on a protracted tour of Europe in September 1823. In Munich he was presented to the King of Bavaria and hailed as "*a new Mozart*" and a pianist equal to the best. Soon Liszt was in Paris where he applied to study at the Conservatoire. The Principal, Cherubini (an Italian!), refused to by-pass a rule that said that foreigners could not be admitted, but Liszt's recitals confirmed his reputation as a genius and led to a great social and commercial success. His ability to improvise was astounding. While there have always been child prodigies, it was generally recognised that the young Liszt was in a class of his own, already the most gifted pianist in the world and also the owner of a prodigious memory.

The family developed a relationship with Pierre Erard, the piano-maker, and soon had access to state-of-the-art instruments with the new double-escapement action that allowed greater control and virtuosity. London followed. Erard provided a new piano and took the opportunity to accompany the Liszts. Liszt performed for two hours for King George IV at Windsor and the king told Adam Liszt: "*This is quite unlike anything I have ever heard. This boy surpasses Moscheles, Cramer, Kalkbrenner and all the other great players, not only in the actual playing but in the wealth and development of his ideas too.*" There were repeated visits to England as the family used Paris as its base over the next four years, although Anna Maria was to return to Austria in 1825.

Adam Liszt succumbed to typhoid in 1827, a tragic blow for his 15-year-old son. Adam had been a loving father who had guided his son's talents and career both wisely and well. On his deathbed he presciently warned his innocent son (who had led a highly protected existence till then) that women would trouble and dominate his life. It was almost inevitable that his words would come true.

Anna Maria Liszt returned to Paris to provide her support and mother and son set up home together. Liszt continued to give concerts and play in salons, but teaching was his major source of income; the pupils were mainly daughters of the aristocracy. His lifestyle became

71

increasingly chaotic and indulgent and he fell in love for the first time. The object of his affections was one of his pupils, Caroline de Saint-Cricq, the daughter of a government minister, the Comte de Saint-Cricq, who quickly put a stop to their meetings and married her off into a loveless relationship. Liszt was never to forget her and they were to meet again many years later.

Liszt suffered a nervous breakdown in 1828. He turned to religion and, like his father before him, wanted to become a priest. He became seriously ill and rumours of his death were rampant to the extent that his obituary was published in one Paris newspaper. During this crisis he composed little, choosing instead to immerse himself in literature.

It took the three-day revolution of 1830 to snap Liszt out of his depression and he was prominent in the artistic renaissance that quickly flourished. Influenced by his extensive reading, this highly intelligent youth developed a strong social conscience. He was attracted by the ideas of the Comte de Saint-Simon which focused on improving the lot of the poor. His circle was thus both artistic and radical.

Paris was now a thriving musical centre. Liszt attended the premiere of Berlioz's *Symphonie Fantastique* and thus a close and life-long friendship started. The virtuoso violinist Paganini created his usual sensation on his arrival in Paris, inspiring Liszt with his virtuosity and sense of theatre. Liszt attended Chopin's first Paris concert and they became friends and mutual admirers. Mendelssohn, also a member of this extraordinary coterie of musical geniuses, was astounded when Liszt played the former's *Piano Concerto in G minor* by sight from Mendelssohn's hardly legible manuscript.

Liszt's love-life, complicated by the number of women who fell for his fame, very considerable charm and good looks, took a dramatic new direction in 1833 when he met Marie, Comtesse d'Agoult, at a Parisian soirée. She was married to a French aristocrat 15 years her elder by whom she had two young daughters. She was rich, intelligent and beautiful and had been described as "*six inches of snow on 20 feet of lava*". In time many people remarked how she and Liszt were "*so similar in height, in colour of eyes and hair, in complexion and voice, people took us for brother and sister.*" An intense relationship developed, but the couple stopped seeing each other in the early summer of 1834. Liszt spent the summer staying with the Abbé Félicité de Lamennais, a leading spiritual figure and writer, and turned his mind to composing. Lamennais described Liszt as having: *"one of the most beautiful and noble souls that I have met on this earth."*

Marie's elder daughter died at the end of 1834 and when she came out of the ensuing deep depression she renewed the relationship with Liszt and quickly fell pregnant. The couple disappeared to Switzerland and settled in Geneva, leaving behind a *"grande scandale"*. A daughter, Blandine, was born in December 1835, another daughter, Cosima, was born two years later and a son, Daniel, was born in 1839.

The novelist George Sand, a member of their Paris circle, joined them for a summer holiday in Chamonix in 1836. The event, which has been well recorded, is notable for its insight into Liszt's lifestyle at this time. With women dressed in men's clothes, much smoking of pipes and cigars, copious supplies of punch, regular singing and frequent arguing there was much to scandalise the other guests in the hotel. A few months later Liszt made the fateful introduction of George Sand to Chopin.

Liszt visited France several times during 1836 and judged that the scandal of his affair had died down sufficiently to enable the couple to return to Paris in October. While he had been in Geneva a new virtuoso, Sigismund von Thalberg, had filled Liszt's place in Paris. A great rivalry – with much mud-slinging – ensued between the two men. Thalberg gave a recital at the Conservatoire and Liszt responded by hiring, and filling, the Opéra. The denouément came when both virtuosos were invited by Princess Belgiojoso to play at a charity soirée. The princess's conclusion has gone into folklore *"There is only one Thalberg in Paris, but there is only one Liszt in the world"*.

In the following year Liszt discovered Italy and thus began a life-long love affair with the country. In the spring of 1838 he was with Marie in Venice but he rushed off to Vienna, leaving her behind, responding to an urgent appeal from Hungary where the Danube had burst its banks and caused great devastation and loss of life. Liszt gave a number of concerts to raise urgently needed funds and his reputation soared even higher. Here he met the pianist Clara Wieck, soon to be married to Robert Schumann. Clara's father, her teacher, found that Liszt *"can be compared to no other player – he stands alone."* Clara kept Schumann informed and he was soon sending Liszt copies of his piano compositions, including the dedication of the *Fantasie in C*. Liszt and Schumann did not however meet until 1840.

The concerts in Vienna determined Liszt to concentrate on concert performance for the immediate years ahead and to turn his back on domestic life. Thus the greatest and most famous pianist of the time gave hundreds of performances over the next eight years, covering Europe from Spain to Ireland, from Russia to Turkey. In England he played from Ryde to Preston, from Leamington to Ipswich, with audiences ranging from 30 to 400. Liszt had an extremely wide repertoire including many arrangements of other composers' works. The schedule was punishing, and some of the incidents hair-raising! Music "groupies" were in existence even in those days and an attractive woman would sometimes join the party for an indeterminate period.

One highlight of this period was his return to Hungary at the end of 1839, when he was presented with a jewelled sabre and accorded an amazing reception. The streets of Pest were filled with admirers. Another was an extraordinary reception in Berlin in 1842 where he gave numerous concerts. He left the city with his friend Prince Lichnowsky in a carriage drawn by six white horses, leading a procession of hundreds of other carriages and coaches, saluted by the King and Queen of Prussia. *Lisztomania* was the word created to describe the extraordinary response that Liszt generated, the first example of what today is a frequent phenomenon.

Other important events of this period included Liszt's appointment in 1842 as Kapellmeister at the Court of the Grand Duke of Saxe-Weimar-Eisenach in Weimar, where Bach and the poets Goethe and Schiller had previously received patronage. His responsibilities were flexible until he was to settle there six years later. By now his long periods of absence and well-known affairs with numerous women had soured his relationship with Marie. Liszt arranged for their children to live with his mother and in 1843 Marie started to write a novel intended to denigrate Liszt by association.

In 1845 Liszt played a major role in the long-awaited unveiling of a statue of Beethoven in Bonn. Without Liszt's generosity neither the statue nor the attendant festival would have taken place. The concerts were scheduled to take place in a riding school with appalling acoustics, and Liszt paid for a special temporary hall to be erected in just ten days.

It was in Bonn that Liszt first became aware of an Irish adventuress who went under the name of Lola Montez. She was determined to seduce Liszt and was to cause him much trouble.

By 1846 the relationship with Marie was over and Liszt, to his distress and anger, learned of the novel. The seeds of the next significant emotional relationship in Liszt's life were sown in 1847 when he was in Kiev. There he met the 28-year-old Princess Carolyne von Sayn-Wittgenstein, an enormously rich admirer. She was an eccentric and plain woman, religious, extremely well-read but obsessive. She had been the only child of extremely wealthy parents and was now separated from her husband. She lived with her daughter on an enormous estate at Woronince in Russian-controlled Poland. She fell totally in love with Liszt and he responded in kind.

Tiring of the exhausting schedule of the professional virtuoso and influenced by the new relationship with Carolyne, Liszt brought down the curtain on his performing career. He never again charged a fee for playing the instrument of which he was the greatest exponent. Concerts, except in private, became rare events, and his future was to be primarily as composer and teacher.

Liszt stayed with Carolyne at Woronice over the early winter of 1847/8 before moving on to Weimar which was to be his home for the next 13 years. Later Carolyne left Russia with her daughter to join Liszt. The early months were dominated by the revolutions that started in Paris and spread through much of Europe. Remarkably, Liszt and Carolyne – who planned to liquidate her Polish assets – travelled extensively. Liszt had hopes that Hungary would find freedom, and even visited the barricades in Vienna, but the old order was to prevail.

The reasonably liberal Weimar was hardly effected by the uprisings and Liszt returned there to fulfil his duties as Kapellmeister and to compose. Carolyne rented a 30-roomed house, the Altenburg, on the outskirts of the town. Liszt sent for his many possessions from Paris, including a spinnet that had belonged to Mozart and a Broadwood piano that had been Beethoven's. Officially Liszt lived in a hotel for the sake of decorum, and initially the Weimar Court turned a blind eye to his liaison. Soon the Altenburg saw a procession of exalted visitors who were royally entertained by Liszt and Carolyne.

Liszt had first started to conduct in 1840 and he now had a great opportunity to develop his skills with a very good, if small, orchestra at his disposal. He played a major role in promoting the operas of Richard Wagner, whom he had met in Dresden. He, more than anyone, recognised Wagner's genius and performed *Tannhäuser* and *The Flying Dutchman*, and gave the premiere of *Löhengrin*. When Wagner fled from the Dresden revolution in which he had played a significant part, Liszt gave him refuge and provided a false passport to get Wagner to Switzerland.

Hector Berlioz, who had found it difficult to have his highly original music performed in Paris, was another to benefit from Liszt's tenure at Weimar. Liszt revived the opera *Benvenuto Cellini* and there were regular Berlioz Festivals. At one of these Liszt premiered his own *E flat concerto* with Berlioz conducting. Whether by coincidence or as the result of feeding from each other, Liszt, Wagner and Berlioz became the greatest interpretive conductors of the mid-nineteenth century.

The Altenburg became a training ground for a new generation of great pianists including Tausig and Hans von Bülow whom Cosima married in 1857. Amongst all Liszt's activities the most important was composing and he created a series of masterpieces including the *Faust Symphony* and the *Sonata in B minor*. In the early years in Weimar some of Liszt's most talented pupils assisted him to orchestrate his works but by 1853 he undertook the task entirely by himself.

Many famous people and musicians visited the Altenburg. The young Brahms was one of them although he did not endear himself to Liszt by falling asleep while Liszt played. Liszt kept a veritable open house that resonated with the performance and creation of great music, the highlights being when he could be persuaded or tricked into playing the piano. His performance of Beethoven's mighty *Hammerklavier Sonata*, which he did so much to bring into the public arena, was the ultimate experience for his pupils and guests.

Liszt had at least one other intimate relationship during this period, Certainly he fell in love with one of his pupils, Agnès Sreet-Klingworth, whose father was a spy. When she left Weimar they continued to meet each other whenever possible. Liszt's professional relationship with the Court at Weimar became increasingly frustrating as money was too short for him to realise his musical ambitions. In addition, Carolyne was barred from the Court as a result of her protracted battle with the Russian Czar to obtain a divorce – the Grand Duchess at Weimar was the Czar's sister! After being barracked by a clique at the opera, Liszt resigned as Kapellmeister in 1859 and two years later an era closed when the Altenburg was locked up.

Liszt aged dramatically over the Weimar years and tragedy struck when his son Daniel died in Berlin in 1859 with Liszt at his side. The composer now sought a new and more peaceful direction. Rome was to be his base for the next seven years and he planned to marry Carolyne there in October 1861. The couple believed that the long battle with the Church to get her marriage annulled had been won, but her relatives who were determined not to lose her estate intervened once more. The moment passed and marriage was never again on Liszt's agenda.

Liszt was desolate when he lost another of his children in 1862. Blandine died of septicaemia two months after giving birth to a son, Daniel. Her husband was to become Prime Minister of France some years later. Anna Liszt had lived with her granddaughter for many years and looked after her great-grandson until she too died in 1866. And Liszt's surviving daughter, Cosima soon gave him much heartache when she started an affair with Wagner and had three children by him.

In June 1863 Liszt moved into the Madonna del Rosario, a peaceful monastery with magnificent views over Rome and the surrounding mountains. He had a small room with just a bed, a table, a bookcase and an upright piano and there he was able to compose. He was visited by Pope Pius IX to whom he played some of his own compositions and some Beethoven. He was also given the permanent use of rooms at the Villa d'Este at Tardi, a secluded and beautiful home which he came to love during his many visits over the years.

By 1865 Liszt had determined to enter the church and he took minor orders – he was now Abbé Liszt – and moved into the Vatican. The cassock was to become his regular dress from then on. Liszt's new role should not be over-estimated – he was only entitled to assist in Church ceremonies and could not give Mass. In reality he continued his life much as previously, and it is notable that celibacy was not required.

August 1865 saw him in Pest in Hungary where he conducted the premiere of his oratorio *St.Elisabeth* and other works. He was feted when he travelled to London and Paris. In Paris he played four-hands with Camille Saint-Saëns and met César Franck again.

He completed his *Christus* and the *Hungarian Coronation Mass*, the latter composed for the coronation in 1867 of the Austrian Emperor and Empress as King and Queen of Hungary – a small step towards greater independence for his homeland. Liszt was considered too nationalistic to conduct his Mass but probably made a greater impact by singing in the chorus. After the concert he left the church and walked to the bridge over the Danube. The scene has been described:

> *An immense multitude was waiting in eager anticipation to see the royal procession which was soon to cross the bridge... It was during these moments of feverish intensity that the tall figure of a priest suddenly appeared. He was dressed in a long black cassock studded with numerous decorations and as he advanced hat in hand, his snow-white hair stirred gently in the breeze and his features seemed cast in brass. At sight of him a murmur arose, which grew in volume as he drew nearer and was recognised. Swift as lightning, the name of Liszt flew from mouth to mouth, from row to row; and soon he was being given frenzied greeting by a hundred thousand men and women intoxicating themselves with enthusiasm expressed in this thunderous vocal hurricane. The crowd on the other side of the river naturally thought it must be the King who was approaching and being acclaimed with spontaneous emotion of a reconciled people. It was not the King, but it was a king, to whom were addressed the sympathies of a grateful nation proud of the possession of such a son.*

In 1867 Liszt visited Wagner at his villa Tribschen. Liszt's displeasure at Cosima's relationship with Wagner did not prevent a famous perform-ance of Wagner's latest opera *Die Meistersinger* where Wagner sang all the vocal parts and Liszt sight-read the vocal score. Three years later Cosima got her divorce from Hans von Bulöw and Wagner became Liszt's son-in-law.

The relationship with Weimar was restored in 1869 and Liszt was given the use of a secluded house, the Hofgärtnerei, by the Grand Duke. Now Liszt started his "*Vie trifurqué*", a tripartite life where he spent a significant part every year in each of the three cities of Rome, Weimar and Budapest. Liszt was typically to spend his summers in Weimar for the rest of his life and the Hofgärtnerei was to become the Mecca for all budding virtuoso pianists. Three afternoons a week Liszt held master-classes, for which the only entry fee was talent and industry, although some less than brilliant pianists, particularly young women, were able to inveigle their way in. Many of the young women fell in love or became besotted with Liszt and this had some dramatic consequences. One ended up having a mental breakdown and another, Olga Janina, threatened to kill both Liszt and herself. Later she wrote a thinly disguised book implying that they had an affair.

In February 1870 the Norwegian composer Edvard Grieg visited Liszt in Rome after Liszt had helped him to obtain a government grant to travel and study abroad. Grieg had the manuscript of his *Piano Concerto* with him and Liszt played it through at sight. Fifty years later Grieg's widow said that she and her husband owed their life's happiness to Liszt.

From 1871 Liszt developed a close relationship with Baroness Olga von Meyendorff, a rich widow and a talented pianist; Carolyne remained in Rome for the rest of her life writing an enormous religious book. Liszt's bonds with his homeland deepened when he was appointed a Royal Hungarian Councillor. Liszt became an icon for his countrymen, for he was now one of the most famous (and controversial) people in Europe. He played a significant role in developing the musical life of his country, including the formation of a music academy.

The remaining months of each year were devoted to Italy where the Villa d'Este was a haven. He still found time to compose and spend time with Cosima and Wagner. One unforgettable evening, Wagner having retired to bed, Liszt was discussing Beethoven's last piano sonatas and ended up performing the *Hammerklavier* incomparably. At the end Wagner came "*thundering down the stairs in his nightshirt and flung his arms round Liszt's neck, sobbing with emotion.*"

Liszt continued to have the greatest admiration for his son-in-law's talents. He subscribed to the Bayreuth Festival and attended many performances there. The two composers last met in Venice in January 1883 when Liszt stayed in Venice with his family. But a month later Wagner was dead and Cosima cut herself off from the world and her father.

During Liszt's last years he was feted wherever he travelled in Europe, often for performances of his orchestral and choral works. He was treated like royalty and would be treated as an equal by princes and Emperors. His public adored him and to see Franz Liszt was a popular ambition – but only the luckiest heard him perform. In 1881 he suffered a fall down stairs from which his health and energy never recovered. Several of his female piano students spent time looking after him and travelling with him, particularly Lina Schmalhausen who was close to him until his death.

On New Year's day in 1886 Liszt said "*You will see, this will be a disastrous year for me because it begins with a Friday*". His eyes started to trouble him and his health was poor. This didn't stop him visiting Paris and London, where he gave some private impromptu recitals. A performance of *St. Elisabeth* was acclaimed and he was invited to Windsor Castle where he played for Queen Victoria, taking his own grand piano. London caught Liszt fever and The Times reported "*Ovations such as those offered to Liszt have never before been witnessed in musical England.*"

In early July Liszt travelled to Bayreuth for the wedding of his grand-daughter Daniella. On July 19 he was in Luxembourg and performed at a concert for what would be the last time. Unwell with a nasty cough and fever, he still insisted on going back to Bayreuth where Cosima needed his support for the festival. He was not invited to stay at Wahnfried, the Wagner home, but had to take a room nearby. He was able to attend performances of *Parsifal* and *Tristan* but then developed a high temperature and inflammation of the lungs. With her daughters Cosima took charge of her father and forbade Liszt's friends to see him. She herself continued to entertain her guests.

Liszt fell into a coma in the early hours of Saturday July 31. Doctors attended him that evening and gave him two injections near the heart. He immediately suffered convulsions and died just before midnight. Cosima arrived shortly afterwards and stayed with her dead father till the morning. The next day Liszt's body was put in a coffin and taken across the street to Wahnfried.

Liszt was buried in the local cemetery on August 3. Many who would have wanted to be there were unable to make it in time. The cortège left from Wagner's house into streets hastily lined with black flags and spectators, Liszt's pupils on either side of the coffin. The next morning a requiem service was held in the Catholic church – the music had received little thought, none of Liszt's music was played, and the only notable point was that Anton Bruckner was the organist. Liszt's grave was soon covered with wreaths from admirers and institutions from all over Europe. But the Bayreuth Festival continued uninterrupted and the flag at the Festspielhaus remained at the top of the pole.

Liszt *The person*

In his youth Liszt was tall, slim and handsome, but with a delicate air. He had long dark hair which he always kept to shoulder length and a long aristocratic nose. He always dressed impeccably and extravagantly – he had an enormous wardrobe. His good looks and his fame made him extremely attractive to women, a temptation he frequently could not resist. In later years his girth broadened, he developed some prominent warts and his hair became snow-white.

He was highly intelligent, an original thinker and innovator, bringing new forms into music (symphonic poem), into teaching (masterclasses) and into performance (the solo recital). He had a prodigious and all-round piano technique and few dispute that he was the greatest pianist of the 19th century if not of all time. His pupil Felix Weingartner wrote in 1936 that *"Liszt's touch was indescribably beautiful."* He had inherent musicality and taste and was a fabulous extemporiser.

Lacking a broad early education he invested much time in making himself well-read and he also became a quite prolific writer (he wrote a biography of Chopin), often in partnership with Marie or Carolyne. He was a romantic, with strong feelings for the oppressed, for his homeland and for the Church.

Liszt had a considerable fondness for brandy (in later life he would drink a bottle a day), loved good cigars, a game of whist and, of course, attractive or aristocratic women. In an age when divorce was anathema, he did not abide by society's rules and some of the women he got involved with created scandals that reverberated throughout Europe. He inspired deep loyalty amongst his pupils.

As a performer he could indulge in showmanship but, far more important, he was capable of performing and interpreting music in a way that left many who heard him in no doubt that he was incomparable.

Liszt had an extraordinarily generous nature. This was shown in the way that he gave free tuition to pupils, charity concerts for the poor and disadvantaged, or support for fellow composers who were struggling. He even continued to support colleagues, whether composers or performers, who turned against his music or his way of life. It was inevitable that an artist with such a high profile and lifestyle should have his detractors and he bore their criticism with dignity.

He was a democrat and was truly international in outlook. He had a gift for diplomacy, great charm and humanity and was inherently honest and decent. Many spoke of his noble character. On the other hand he had his bad days and could be devastatingly rude to students who were not up to the mark.

By the last years of his life he had become one of the best loved and admired people in Europe as much for the strength of his personality and character as for his prowess as a pianist. He was arguably the greatest human being amongst composers

Liszt *His Music*

Franz Liszt's reputation as a composer has been unjustly over-shadowed by his fame as a performing artist. Unlike Chopin his creativity as a composer extended beyond the piano, he composed in most genres, bringing to each his unwillingness to be bound to classical form. The symphonic poem was a genre he created and his piano miniatures in particular opened new vistas in the Romantic age. He had a profound influence on his son-in-law Wagner. He spans an extraordinary era having met Beethoven and taught Weingartner, the famous conductor who died in 1942.

Liszt was highly prolific and also played a leading role in bringing other composer's music to European audiences through transcriptions, paraphrases and fantasies ranging from the Beethoven and Berlioz symphonies to the best known operas of the day. The piano music is so extensive that much of it is never heard in the concert hall and some has only recently been recorded for the first time. There is a wealth of riches to be discovered in Liszt's music.

Deciding on the "Liszt Starter Pack" is not easy as there are so many candidates:

1 Liebestraum No.3 makes an ideal introduction. It is a short piece for piano, initially dream-like, with a glorious melody – you may well know it.

2 Italie (Years of pilgrimage Vol.2) shows Liszt's pianism on a much larger canvas, using art and literature as its inspiration. It opens with *Sposalizio*, inspired by Raphael's painting *The marriage of the Virgin*. With its simple but memorable three-note main theme, it is a contemplative and beautiful work. It is followed by *Il Penseroso*, inspired by a Michelangelo statue, a moving melancholic piece. The three *Petrarch Sonnets*, originally songs, are gorgeous pieces, particularly *104*, running the complete range of emotions from tranquillity to elevated passion. *Après une lecture du Dante*, also known as the *Dante Sonata*, is a response to the poet's *Inferno*, a powerful, dramatic and virtuosic work, enthralling to hear.

3 Faust Symphony Based on Goethe's great work, the first movement depicts Faust himself, Liszt revealing his character and circumstances through some of his most memorable themes and some great love music for Gretchen. She is the subject of the ravishing second movement which opens with gentle flutes and clarinets. Serene and delicate, her music symbolically melts Faust's themes. *Mephistopheles* is the scherzo movement, given the marking *allegro vivace ironico*, brilliant, pungent music that distorts the Faust themes. Ultimately Gretchen's theme triumphs – exquisite horn and cello – and trombones intone a quiet chorale. Out of silence comes the last movement, a male chorus singing, *andante mistico*, *"Alles Vergängliche ist nur ein Gleichnis"* (*Everything transitory is only approximation*), the same passage used by Mahler to close his *Symphony No.8*. A tenor joins the chorus to take the music to a superbly uplifting and mighty conclusion.

4 Piano Concerto No.1 Few concertos have such an arresting opening, majestic with a simple but memorable theme. It has many exquisite and delicate touches between the excitement of the virtuoso passages. The second movement *quasi adagio* is again instantly memorable, before the cellos briefly interrupt the communion. The triangle introduces the playful *allegretto vivace* before grinding cellos and basses lead into a return of the opening theme for full orchestra, this time with brass dominant, to launch the finale. This majestic theme alternates with a perky theme in march-time, building to a rousing climax.

Orchestral Music

Liszt wrote a series of twelve symphonic poems, a term that he introduced after the first few had seen the light of day as overtures. All take their inspiration from literary works except one, which is inspired by a painting. Between 15 and 30 minutes long, they are highly enjoyable. Start with *Les Préludes*, which has a memorable and energising motto theme that contrasts with a yearning second theme. The former drives forward, the latter consoles and the work has a brilliant conclusion, drums, cymbals and trumpets prominent.

Orpheus celebrates the god of music in a noble outpouring, harp prominent. Liszt uses one great theme in highly creative ways in *Tasso, Lamento e Trionfo* In the first section there are intimate and beautiful passages leading to a thrilling, trumpet-led climax. The middle section has the theme in all its magnificence, but in a gentle minuet, and the concluding *Trionfo* has the theme radiant, the final bars worthy of a national anthem.

Ce qu'on entend sur la montagne was the first in the series. It opens with a mystery and rapture that surely influenced Wagner in writing *Tristan und Isolde* – thrilling! Next there is a powerful declamatory theme, strings with trumpet fanfares. A tempestuous passage is followed by a passage of calm, gentle strokes on the gong introducing solo instruments, the violin radiant; but this does not last for long and a restless mood returns. A sombre trombone chorale leads to the conclusion, where the main themes fight it out triumphantly, only for Liszt to add an epilogue in reflective vein.

In the remaining symphonic poems you will find more highly enjoyable music.

Piano Concerto No.2 is a very different work from its predecessor, it has a gentle woodwind opening before the piano enters a hushed atmosphere and articulates different chords with singing violins and cellos before a horn-call ramps up the excitement. The piano sets off on a great journey, basses prominent in the trudging accompaniment, dramatic and demonic in the main until breaking gently into the swooning strings of the second movement. A solo cello is soon holding the piano enraptured, a most moving, chamber-music-like passage before cascades of notes from the piano lead to a thrilling grand march for the orchestra. This is magnificent entertainment and I can imagine Liszt dispatching this concerto imperiously. The tension drops for a chamber interlude before a brief barnstorming conclusion.

Totentanz (Danse Macabre) is a paraphrase on the *Dies Irae* for piano and orchestra. It is one of Liszt's most futuristic works and you could easily believe it was composed in the 20th century rather than around 1850. A set of six variations, which range from gentle to violent, the piano part is brilliant, the overall effect dramatic and enthralling.

The *Dante Symphony*, a powerful work in three movements, was inspired by the poet's *Divine Comedy*. It opens with *Inferno*, a vivid depiction of hell to rhythmic, rich music, macabre at times. A cor anglais introduces a plaintive section recalling the forbidden love of Francesca da Rimini which breaks into an *andante amoroso* singing with passion. But harps warn, and hell is conjured up by the orchestra – trombones chanting, cymbals, the lot, building to a terrifying climax and hammer blows. *Purgatorio*, in four sections, is a long song of melancholy, but beautiful and much more consoling than one might expect. The *lamentoso* section is in the form of a fugue, building to a heady climax before its conclusion. The *Magnificat* provides a final benediction, a female chorus first, then a radiant soprano to conclude with powerful organ chords provided by the orchestra before harps and "*Hosannas*" provide a radiant close.

Piano Music

The piano music of Liszt is of the very highest order and of great accessibility. The *Hungarian Rhapsodies* are a brilliant series of 19 pieces for piano, each typically five to ten minutes long, which also exist in orchestral versions. They are virtuoso works in either format and should be heard in both. They combine beautiful and vital themes with magical effects and passion. Start with *No.2 in C sharp minor* which opens with its slow formalities; but the bells are soon pealing and we are off on a thrilling gypsy ride before breaking into the famous theme that you will recognise – brilliant and enormous fun. *No.12* opens with drum rolls out of which emerge a gorgeous lilting melody that soon conjures up a picture of gypsy dancing. Soon we are introduced to the lilting melody as a great aria before the piece cascades to a climax, all themes bundled in. *No.15* is Liszt's arrangement of the famous Rákóczy March, beloved by all Hungarians. Liszt does weird and wonderful things with it, rivalling the Berlioz version. These are just some of the *Rhapsodies*, do hear them all.

The *Sonata in B minor* is one of the mighty classics of the piano repertoire and its virtuosity, strength and beauty are quite staggering. In this continuous three-movement work Liszt uses six main themes which have many transformations. It opens quietly and starkly but soon launches into the *allegro agitato assai*, the piano raging and leaving you wondering how the pianist's fingers can be creating the notes and how the piano can withstand the onslaught. The slow movement provides peace and tranquillity that leads into a noble and passionate outpouring before subsiding. Finally we are off on a roller-coaster of a fugue before the music sensationally builds to two mighty climaxes in double octaves. Boldly Liszt decides to have a quiet and spiritual conclusion, the music like a prayer, gradually dying away, ending on a low B, the note that began the work.

Liszt's *Douze Grandes Etudes* are jaw-dropping! They are the more difficult 1837 predecessors of the 1851 *Douze Etudes d'exécution transcendante*. These are stunning virtuosic pieces that at the time were virtually unplayable by anyone other than Liszt. *No.4* has simplicity and brilliance, *No.5* is light as a feather, *No.8* has a velocity of notes that is almost unbelievable, *No.9* is an exquisite *andantino*, a welcome respite before the magnificence, brilliance and drive of *No.10* whose conclusion assaults the piano. In *No.11* the theme grows in majesty in an exhilarating way before ebbing away into silence. In the concluding *No.12* tremolos surround the simple and plaintive theme on its transformation.

The complete *Années de pèlerinage* is a set of three volumes, *Suisse, Italie* (see the Starter Pack) and *Troisième Année*, each volume containing between seven and ten pieces. *Suisse* opens with *Chapelle de Guillaume Tell*, a glorious portrait of the Swiss national hero. Its haunting theme is memorable, the music poetic, dramatic and heroic in turn. It ensures you have to hear what follows. Next we have *Au lac du Wallenstadt*, the water lapping against a melancholy melody. *Pastorale* is a brief, gentle dancing piece. *Au bord d'une source (Beside a spring)* has cascades of rippling delicacy. *Orage (Storm)* is suitably virtuosic. The set ends with *Les Cloches de Genève*, a nocturne with quiet bells pealing.

Troisième Année is the serious volume, it was written much later than the others and shows how Liszt's style became more progressive. It opens with *Angelus!*, subtitled *Prayer to the Guardian Angels*, which is an evocation of the bells Liszt heard in Rome. Next come three pieces evoking the Villa d'Este, the first two, inspired by the enormous cypresses, are profound, the third, inspired by the magnificent fountains, is a veritable cascade. Among the remaining three pieces is a formidable *Marche Funèbre*.

Amongst the hundreds of piano works make sure you listen to the following. The *Mephisto Waltz No. 1* is a work of stunning virtuosity that carries you along in its diabolical and seductive brilliance. The *Berceuse (S174b)* is based on Chopin's *Berceuse* and is a beautiful threnody. *La Campanella* is a brilliant tribute to Paganini

Funérailles, No. 7 from the *Harmonies Poétiques et religieuses* is a heroic lament for Hungarians killed in the 1848-9 Revolution. It opens with thundering power that gives way to a haunting dead march. When consolation comes it is like balm. From the same set *Bénédiction de Dieu* is a work of great beauty, consolation again a key theme.

In the two *St. Francis Légendes* Liszt's imagery is extraordinary. The first, *St. Francis of Assisi: Preaching to the birds*, has exquisite depiction of birdsong alongside the poetic main themes. In *St. Francis of Paola walking on the water* Liszt conjures up a veritable storm before a triumphant conclusion.

As an encore piece the *Grand Galop Chromatique (S219)* is perfect, brilliant to the point of being outrageous.

Liszt's transcriptions and paraphrases (the latter allowing more poetic license) played an important role in bringing great music of the day to a much wider audience. But they are unique works of art in their own right because of Liszt's genius and good taste. For an introduction to what Liszt can do with other composers' music listen to his *Rigoletto: paraphrase de concert*. Liszt brings his inimitable sorcery to the famous quartet from *Act 3* of Verdi's opera. Next try *Réminiscences de Don Juan* from Mozart's opera, again a sheer delight, particularly in its use of *Là ci darem la mano*. Bellini's *Norma* and Wagner's *Tristan und Isolde* are just two more examples in a rich portfolio of unique entertainment from opera.

A special delight are the transcriptions of many of Schubert's songs. Liszt was a great admirer of Schubert and his interpretations are done with love and flair. Start with *Die Forelle (The Trout)* to see what I mean. The dramatic *Erlkönig* was a regular feature in Liszt's concert-making.

Other famous paraphrases include the Beethoven *Symphonies* and the *Symphonie Fantastique* of Berlioz, well worth hearing to appreciate a different aspect of Liszt.

Songs

Liszt wrote more than 80 songs, often in more than one version, and he transcribed some for the piano alone. They are well worth exploring, Liszt's choice of texts was excellent and his brilliant tone-painting skills produced many gems. In *O lieb, so lang du lieben kennst (Oh love, as long as you are able)* you will find the famous melody of *Liebestraum No.3*. In the glorious *Ich möchte hingehn (I would depart)* there lies the original inspiration for the famous love theme from Wagner's *Tristan und Isolde*.

Choral

Christus is Liszt's oratorio, and is an enormous work which lasts for nearly three hours. Little known, it inevitably suffers from the low current interest in oratorios, and from its length. It is in three sections, *Christmas Oratorio* (sometimes performed separately), *After Epiphany, and Passion and Resurrection*. In the *Christmas Oratorio* there are three orchestral movements, *Stabat Mater speciosa* for unaccompanied chorus, and also movements with full orchestral and vocal forces. There is much lovely music. In *After Epiphany* the chorus appears in all sections, some with organ, some with orchestra. *Tu es Petrus* for male chorus is totally arresting in its dramatic presentation, as is the storm scene in *The Miracle*, followed by the magic of the ensuing calm. *Passion and Resurrection* is sad and sombre music until the final minutes when the *Easter Hymn* is sung. In a fugue sounding like pealing bells the cymbals, full choir and orchestra provide the crowning glory of the work.

Liszt's *Motets*, like those of Bruckner, are written in the style of the Renaissance. Typically unaccompanied, they are expressive and rich in harmony and a pleasure to listen to. *Pater Noster 1. Das Vater Unser* is particularly beautiful, the haunting *Ave Verum Corpus* is very different to Mozart's and the *Ave Maria* of 1852, with organ accompaniment, is melodic and memorable.

In a similar style is *Via Crucis (The Way of the Cross)* which sets the 14 Stations of the Cross. We are transported back centuries for this too, except when the organ explodes on the scene. Masterly, and displaying a different side of Liszt!

Organ Music

Liszt became particularly interested in the organ when he settled in Weimar. As you can imagine some sensational works were produced when Liszt brought his creativity, originality and brilliance to the instrument. The *Fantasia and Fugue on the chorale "Ad nos, ad salutarem"* is stunning, half-an-hour long, its theme taken from Meyerbeer's opera, *Le Prophète*. You can hear the trumpet fanfares in the first section and the second, *adagio*, has a gorgeous adaptation of the theme. The concluding *fuga* builds to an awesome climax.

Weinen, Klagen, Sorgen, Zagen is a set of variations on a theme from Bach's cantata of that name. The mood is of sadness and ultimately of consolation as it winds up to a final chorale, the music highly evocative.

Don't miss the *Evocation à la Chapelle Sixtine* where Liszt pays homage to Allegri and Mozart; the music recalls how Mozart copied down Allegri's *Miserere* when he attended the Sistine Chapel as a boy. Liszt uses the *Miserere* and Mozart's *Ave verum corpus* as the basis of a highly moving work.

The *Prelude and fugue on BACH* is a grand fantasy, guaranteed to blow your socks off. It has been described as *"a more or less direct link between Bach and Schoenberg."*

6

FAURÉ

Fauré *His Life*

Gabriel-Urbain Fauré was born on May 12, 1845, in Pamiers in the very south-west of France. He was the youngest of six children – five sons and a daughter – born to Toussaint-Honoré Fauré and his wife. He was an unwanted child and was initially dispatched to a wet-nurse. Toussaint-Honoré was an assistant inspector of primary schools and a few years after Fauré's birth he was appointed to run a teachers' training college near Foix, a nearby town.

The young Fauré had a rather lonely existence and his one real pleasure was to play the harmonium in the college chapel. An old blind lady gave him some basic instructions but he worked things out for himself so successfully that by the age of eight he was recognised as having a talent. A family friend suggested that Fauré should attend a new school of religious music in Paris and a year later Toussaint-Honoré agreed.

The nine-year-old Fauré left his family and arrived in Paris in October 1854 to attend Louis Niedermeyer's School of Classical and Religious Music. Niedermeyer had worked with Rossini and was an excellent pianist. Pupils were allowed out of the small school only on Sundays, and then only with a designated guardian. The regime was rigorous but fair and provided an excellent grounding in music, with an emphasis on the piano, organ and singing. The school was spartan, the roof leaked, there were fifteen pianos crowded into one room and the food was basic. The best senior pupils were used as additional teachers for the juniors.

Niedermeyer became a father figure for Fauré, who was the director's favourite pupil, but he died in 1861. A less popular teacher was appointed to replace him and the piano-teaching role was taken on by the 26-year-old Camille Saint-Saëns, a gifted pianist and ambitious composer. The two formed a friendship that lasted until Saint-Saëns's death in 1921. Fauré visited Saint-Saëns's home regularly on a Sunday to enjoy his older friend's mother's cooking and she became Fauré's official guardian.

The main interest of Fauré's early life was inevitably the piano, but by the age of 16 he was composing seriously and entering the school's annual competition. He finally won in his last year when he was 20, probably with the *Cantique de Jean Racine*. The previous year he had had to seek retrospective permission from the great writer Victor Hugo after setting some of his songs to music.

Fauré's headmaster helped his departing pupil by finding him a position as an organist at the church of St. Sauveur in Rennes, a town in Brittany over 200 miles from Paris. Life in provincial France had its moments − thanks to a lively group of young teachers at the main school. Less sympathetic was Fauré's priest who objected to his organist leaving the organ loft during his sermon to have a cigarette outside, and to his arrival for early morning mass in evening dress, straight from a ball!

Saint-Saëns remained in contact, ready to advise his young friend. He helped Fauré to find a publisher in Paris and at the end of 1869, concerned that Fauré was out of the mainstream in Rennes, he alerted him to a vacant organist's position at Clignancourt in Paris. Saint-Saëns was by now making a name for himself and thus on his return to the capital Fauré had an immediate entrée to a stimulating musical scene. In a letter he referred to having heard the famous pianist Rubinstein performing at "grandfather's", as he jokingly referred to Saint-Saëns. Life was severely disrupted by the Franco-Prussian war of 1870. Fauré enlisted in the infantry and participated in the defence of Paris. He came under fire and was awarded a medal.

After the armistice Fauré spent the summer of 1871 as a teacher at the Niedermeyer school which had decamped temporarily to the founder's old home in Switzerland. Fauré returned to Paris with the school in the autumn and took on the position of organ accompanist at St. Sulpice where Charles Widor was the organist. He was quite prepared to deputise for Saint-Saëns who was organist at La Madeleine when the latter was giving recitals elsewhere.

Saint-Saëns was a leading light in the creation in 1871 of the Société Nationale de Musique, formed to bring together for concerts the progressives amongst the young composers and musicians of Paris. The other composers included Franck, d'Indy and Lalo. Saint-Saëns would play piano duets with Fauré and there were opportunities for new works to be heard. A symphony by Fauré was premiered in 1874 but the composer was dissatisfied and withdrew it.

Fauré was a late developer as a composer and his first masterpiece, his *Violin Sonata No. 1*, was not written until he was 30. It was written at the Brittany country home of Camille Clerc, a friend whose much younger wife had become a confidant of Fauré. Clerc ensured that the *Violin Sonata No. 1* was published by the leading German publishing house of Breitkopf and Härtel. This was a coup for Fauré who was quite happy to forego any royalties because of the prestige. The *Piano Quartet No. 1* soon followed.

Amongst the salons that Fauré had gained access to was that of Pauline Viardot, one of the great French singers of her day. He fell in love with her daughter Marianne and pursued a long courtship. Mme. Viardot introduced Fauré to Charles Gounod. Through the efforts of Gounod and Clerc, Fauré was appointed Maitre de Chapelle at the Madeleine in 1877, a position he was to hold until 1896. He still needed to give piano lessons in order to survive financially.

Marianne Viardot and Fauré became engaged in July 1877. Fauré was passionate about Marianne but she began to find him too intense and in the words of her mother *"fell out of love"*. The engagement was broken off, and heartbroken, Fauré took himself off to Weimar with Camille Clerc to attend the premiere of Saint-Saëns' *Samson and Delilah* which had been sponsored by Franz Liszt. When Fauré met the pianist and composer, the great man played part of Fauré's *Ballade* and gave him valuable advice. Liszt henceforth retained an interest in Fauré's compositions.

In April 1879 Fauré traveled to Cologne with another friend, the young composer André Messager, to hear Richard Wagner's Ring operas, *Das Reingold* and *Die Walküre*. In the autumn they visited Munich to hear the complete Ring cycle. Fauré admired some of Wagner's operas greatly; he was less impressed by others, including *Tristan* and *Tannhaüser*. Unusually for a young composer at that time, his works were little influenced by Wagner. The next few years were taken up with composing, including an aborted violin concerto, and musical trips in Europe, including another visit to Liszt in 1882.

Fauré wanted to get married. One of his close friends and female admirers, Marguerite Baugnies, and her mother assisted him in choosing his future bride. Apparently the names of three girls judged suitable were put in a hat and Fauré drew out that of Marie Fremiet, the daughter of a well-known sculptor who was an ambitious artist in her own right. Mme Baugnies and her mother visited the Fremiets and the couple were introduced. They married in March 1883 and had a son Emmanuel in December; a second son, Phillippe arrived six years later. Fauré was to become close to his father-in-law.

Fauré, recognising the need to make money and that opera was the only way to achieve this, spent much time on finding a suitable libretto but with no success. However he did the next best thing, over the next decade he was to write incidental music for a number of plays.

Fauré liked to have intimate relationships with admiring women. Marie Clerc and Marguerite Baugnies were two of the earliest, but a key figure was Winnie Singer, daughter of the American sewing machine millionaire, Isaac Singer. Winnie's mother was French and when widowed she returned to France. Winnie was a passionate music lover but had studied painting – where she met Marie Fremiet. She first met Fauré through the Clercs and the friendship continued during her first marriage, her divorce, and then her subsequent marriage to the elderly Prince de Polignac. Her husband had status, she had beauty, youth and money, and between them they created the premiere salon in Paris.

Winnie, as Princesse de Polignac, received the dedication of Fauré's *Cinq Mélodies* after he had spent time with her in Venice. He fell deeply under her spell for a while. Life in Paris settled into a round of teaching the piano and attending weekly soirées at the salons of Saint-Saëns, the Viardots, Marguerite Baugnies and the Polignacs.

In 1885 Fauré's father died and he commenced work on the *Requiem*. Before it was complete his mother was also dead. The *Requiem*, in its initial form, had its premiere at the Madeleine in 1888, its reflective style making little impact. Fauré was still little known even at this stage, in large part due to his modest and retiring nature. But he had a wide range of contacts, and not just in music – Marcel Proust, the writer, was a great admirer and Fauré features in his novels.

Fauré's marriage was not a success, his wife Marie was frustrated in her artistic ambitions (she painted scenes onto fans) and Fauré excluded her from much of his life. He would go out alone in the evenings, leaving her at home, increasingly absorbed in bringing up their two sons. Fauré was unfaithful to Marie; he had a major affair with Emma Bardac in the early 1890s. She was 30, married with children for whom Fauré wrote his famous *Dolly Suite*. Emma went on to have an affair with Claude Debussy, by whom she had a daughter before later marrying him.

In 1892 Saint-Saëns persuaded Fauré to apply for a position at the Conservatoire. Ambroise Thomas, the director, is reputed to have responded, *"Fauré? Never, if he's appointed I resign!"* It wasn't until Thomas died four years later that Fauré was successful. In the meantime Fauré was appointed as an Inspector of Musical Education which enabled him to give up his private teaching. The position required much travelling around France. He also undertook several concert tours, including visits to London and Switzerland.

The late 1890s saw the publication of the incidental music for the play *Pelléas et Mélisande* as well as a number of piano works. Fauré was also commissioned to write a lyric tragedy, *Promethée*, for the Béziers Festival of 1900. It involved 800 performers and, in spite of a violent storm nearly destroying the open-air set, it was a great success and had an audience of 10,000 people. Around this time he met the young pianist Marguerite Hasselmans who became his lover and companion for the rest of his life, as well as his preferred interpreter of the piano works.

Fauré was appointed Professor of Composition at the Ecole Niedermeyer in 1901 and became music critic for *le Figaro* in 1903. Between these appointments he started to experience the onset of serious deafness. He also suffered a crisis of confidence in his composing when he took stock of all that was going on around him in France. He composed almost nothing in 1903.

When his pupil Maurice Ravel was not allowed to compete for the Prix de Rome in 1905 the resulting scandal resulted in the resignation of the Director of the Conservatoire, Théodore Dubois. Fauré had championed Ravel's cause and was astonished when he was offered the post of Director in order to bring a fresh approach. Within a few months he introduced plans to reform the traditional Conservatoire and because of his zeal earned himself the nickname "Robespierre".

Three years later another honour fell to Fauré when he was elected to the Institute through the influence of Saint-Saens and Fremiet. He travelled regularly to England and Germany for performances of his works and found time to write the opera he had at last decided on, *Pénélope*. Two outstanding pianists, Alfred Cortot and Marguerite Long, started to include Fauré's music in their repertoire, and a new publisher, Heugel, demanded a regular supply of new works.

Pénélope was eventually premiered in Monte Carlo in March 1913 with a Paris production two months later. Fauré's last visit to England in 1914 was for a performance of all his piano music by one of his former students, Robert Lortat. Some years earlier Lortat had presented himself to Fauré, offering to play any of his piano works, all learned by heart.

The outbreak of the Great War in August 1914 found Fauré trapped in Germany, necessitating a return to France via Switzerland. He spent the war years carrying out his job diligently and composing the *Violin Sonata No. 2* and the *Cello Sonata No. 1* amongst other works. After the war ended Fauré was asked to step down as Director of the Conservatoire because of his deafness and increasing ill-health. He gave his last concert in Tours in 1921 aged 76.

Saint-Saens died in 1922 at the age of 86, ending a close relationship that had lasted over 60 years. A highlight of Fauré's twilight years was a festival of his music in 1922 at the Sorbonne with famous performers including Pablo Casals and Alfred Cortot. His summers were spent at Annecy-le-Vieux with Marguerite. Fauré completed his *Piano Trio* in 1923 and then commenced a *String Quartet* which he successfully completed, not without a struggle.

In September 1924 the ageing composer caught double pneumonia and returned to Paris and his family the following month. He died at 1.50 a.m. on November 4, 1924. Fauré was given a State Funeral attended by the President of the Republique. His own music, including the *Elégie*, was played before the coffin was taken to the cemetery at Passy.

Fauré *The person*

Fauré was shortish, rather rotund, with *"a short strong nose and an obstinate chin"*. He had a tanned complexion and dark eyes. His expression was often melancholy and he had a soft, deep voice. His hair was thick, black when he was young, and increasingly greying from his forties. For most of his life he had a moustache.

He tended to be indolent and lacked application. He found composing difficult, *"like a sticking door that I have to open"*. His adolescence seemed to continue beyond the normal age for growing up. He could be very solitary and quiet, but he might be composing in his head at the time.

He had a good sense of humour but was deeply introspective and *"a feminine type without being in the least effeminate"*. He had great charm which women found enormously appealing. He became a very subtle Don Juan, sensual and passionate, and found the social scene in Paris very intoxicating. He had many friends, some of his most intimate and long-lasting friendships being with women. He made few enemies but in the salons his vanity could cause him to lose sight of those who were his true friends.

He dressed formally and correctly, and operated in the best French style of the time – behaving impeccably with married male friends but perhaps having an affair with their wives.

Fauré *His Music*

The composer Albert Roussel described Fauré and his music thus: *"An essentially French genius, he occupied a place apart in the history of music and, without fuss or meaningless gestures, he pointed the way towards marvellous horizons overflowing with freshness and light where our musicians, for many years to come, will hear re-echoing the harmonious sounds of his voice."*

Fauré chose to accentuate the melodic at the expense of the progressive. The music he wrote is highly appealing and is likely to give you much pleasure. For the "Fauré Starter Pack" I recommend the following works to you:

1 Requiem This is easily and justifiably the composer's most popular work. It is quiet and introspective compared with the requiems of Verdi and Berlioz with their stunning settings of the *Dies Irae* that are amongst the most dramatic in all music. *The Requiem* opens and closes with the hushed words *Requiem aeternam* and Fauré's opening theme is full of consolation. The *Sanctus*, with its harp accompaniment and ethereal violin theme, is music for angels and of course the *Pie Jesu* for solo treble or soprano, gently accompanied, is a stroke of genius – radiant, pure and devout. The flowing *Agnus Dei* offers consolation and by the concluding *In Paradisum* there is no fear of death.

2 Pélleas et Mélisande has justly been called Fauré's symphonic masterpiece. It has four movements, the opening *prélude* has great power and particularly rich strings, its horn call presaging a radiant close. The *andantino* is scherzo-like with a wistful oboe and a purposeful beat. You will probably recognise the famous *Siciliano*, with its flute and harp parts prominent and the melody lilting and lovely. The concluding *molto adagio* is magical, almost funereal before it dies away.

3 Piano Quartet No.1 The opening surely intimates that the work is a masterpiece, it has great sweep and all the instruments are beautifully presented. Dramatic, occasionally dream-like, the opening movement rushes onwards only to end as if gently arriving home. The *scherzo* has been memorably described by the pianist Emanuel Ax as "*uncannily reminiscent of an elegant boulevardier sauntering along the streets of Paris. If there is such a thing as 19th century "cool" this is its musical equivalent.*" The trio is brilliant! The *adagio* is beautiful, profound and intense, a glorious movement. The concluding *allegro molto* is exceedingly lyrical and confident, chamber music at its best, never allowing your attention to stray.

Orchestral Music

Fauré described Masques et Bergamesques as "*Music with a somewhat evocative and melancholy – even nostalgic – character.*" An orchestral suite in four movements, the *Ouverture* is ravishing, beautiful and playful, the *menuet*, stately and gentle. A *gavotte* and a *pastorale – andante tranquillo* conclude this delightful throwback.

The *Ballade for Piano and Orchestra* is a mini piano concerto with three sections, unusual in being slow-fast-slow. It is a lovely reflective work, the piano (for the greater part) gently accompanied by the orchestra with at times some significant contributions from flute and cello.

The well-known *Pavane* is another short work. Instantly appealing, it is an elegant work with a memorable theme and delightful orchestration.

The *Elégie* for cello and orchestra is again short, in effect just a slow movement of a cello concerto. Its magical mood is hushed except for a late surge.

The *Dolly Suite* exists in an orchestration of the music for piano duet by a colleague of Fauré. The music of the lilting opening *Berceuse* is famous, the most significant movement is the penultimate, *Tendresse*, a beautiful and loving slow movement. You will probably also recognise the concluding *Le pas Espagnol*. It is appropriately evocative and benefits from having the full orchestral treatment, an ideal concluding concert piece.

Chamber Music

The *Piano Quartet No. 2* is a fitting companion to its predecessor, the opening movement contemplative, sometimes serene, sometimes heartbreaking. The *scherzo* has the piano rushing along, pulling the other instruments in its wake, with more than a touch of fantasy. The *adagio*, apparently inspired by church bells from Fauré's youth, is beautiful music, dreamlike at times. The concluding *allegro molto* is urgent and dramatic, pressing all the way to an exciting ending.

Amongst Fauré's works the *Piano Quintets* are essential listening. Cascading notes from the piano usher in the violin and the other strings to create the opening of *No. 1*. The theme is memorable and sturdy, the marking *molto moderato*. The *adagio* is heartfelt, melancholic and intense. The last movement opens with a scherzo-like passage that tries to grow into a weighty conclusion but doesn't quite make it.

Piano Quintet No. 2 is a gem with a quietly stated first movement of great beauty, the instruments intertwining seriously. Passions are aroused, however. A quick-silver *scherzo* flies by, followed by an *andante* of unusual intensity – resonant and powerful and quite, quite riveting!

The *finale* is fast-flowing and purposeful, the piano bustling until eventually the cello leads its partners to a satisfying conclusion.

The *Piano Trio in D minor* has an opening movement that offers some delightful harmony from the violin and cello. The *andantino* is like a duet for them, the sonorities rich, the mood increasingly ardent until relaxing for the gentle close. The brief *allegro vivo* opens with an emotional declamation for the strings, answered by the piano, before driving forward, ending like pealing bells in the major key.

Violin Sonata No. 1 is an early work in four movements, the opening *allegro molto* is urgent and intense, the second theme a feminine contrast; together they create an enthralling movement. The *andante* has the violin singing a beautiful song, musing, until the conclusion approaches, when there is a surge of emotion. The third movement is fast, witty and entertaining and the last movement raises a storm.

Violin Sonata No. 2 is a late work, its appeal less immediate because of its serious vein. After the urgency of the opening *allegro non troppo* the *andante* contrasts with its melancholic and meditative calm but soon becomes anguished. The concluding movement goes just half-way to being playful.

Cello Sonata No. 1 is a work which displays it provenance in the Great War. The opening *allegro* has a menacing first theme, the second contrasts with calm. The *andante* quotes a theme from the *Requiem* and is a deeply-felt lament. The *finale* has piano and cello in strong conversation together, building to a charged conclusion.

Cello Sonata No. 2 is in happier mood. The first movement has been well described as having *"ecstatic energy"*. The *andante* has its origins in a funeral march but soon opens out into a more elegiac mood and when switching into the major key the music becomes quietly radiant. The concluding *allegro vivo* rushes here and there.

Piano Music

Fauré's piano music is a treasure trove that, unfortunately, few people explore. This is unfortunate because Fauré fulfils the expectation that a great composer who was also a pianist would write marvellous piano music.

Start with the *Nocturnes*, thirteen works composed between 1875 and 1921. In the same spirit as Chopin's set, they range from four to nine minutes in length. They all demand attention and have very different characters, *No. 1* is questing, *No. 2* quietly beautiful, *No. 3* is happy, *No. 4* is contemplative, *No. 5* whimsical, *No. 6* has serenity, *No. 7* is questioning, *No. 8* is like a farewell. The last five *Nocturnes* take on a new dimension, as if with personal programmes, and have a profundity not found earlier in the set. All are in minor keys. Let no one say Fauré wrote only salon music!

The *Barcarolles* cover a period between 1883 and 1921 and show the same variety and development as the *Nocturnes*. They are a delight, initially languid but by the time we get to *No. 5* they are full of complexity and passion. From now on we are dealing with some of the most appealing but serious music of the 20th century. *Barcarolle No. 9* is deeply contemplative, *No. 12* is a complete contrast, back to a happy world.

The *Nine Préludes* were written in 1910 and 1911 and are deeply intimate works. I cannot improve on the words of the music critic Bryce Morrison; "*Bitter and turbulent, ironically teasing and light-hearted, this extraordinary sequence of Préludes exposes the most private feelings to view. And it says much for Fauré's genius that he could express such a dark night of the soul with such unfaltering courage, lack of indulgence and supreme compositional strength.*"

The *Five Impromptus* were written between 1893 to 1910 and inevitably follow the same development as the *Préludes* and *Barcarolles*. The first three are sheer delight, the last two full of deeper emotion.

The *Valse-Caprices*, four in all, are vivacious entertainments in which Fauré is endlessly inventive, taking attentive listeners on a rewarding and constantly surprising journey.

Songs

With his melodic gifts and expressive piano writing, Fauré inevitably wrote some great songs and there are many to explore. Here are a few to start you off.

La bonne chanson was written to texts by Paul Verlaine. The nine songs are all short and offer great variety, *No. 3 La lune blanche luit dans les bois* is beautifully expressive and the set concludes with the playful *L'hiver a passé.* The piano accompaniment, formidable throughout the cycle, is here almost a match for the singer.

Poème d'un jour, Rencontre, Toujours, Adieu are an early set of songs, the middle two sharing passion and urgency. *Adieu* has a touching simplicity and beauty that makes it very attractive and ends the set on a high note in more ways than one.

Other works

Cantique de Jean Racine is a short work for chorus and orchestra and organ. It is an affirmative work growing from quiet beginnings to great sonority before dying away.

Pénélope is Fauré's only opera, rich in melody but hardly known. It is a must for those who recognise Faurés stature as a great composer. The libretto is based on Greek legend, the tale of Queen Pénélope whose husband Ulysses has been long absent, perhaps dead. She has numerous ambitious suitors and has promised to choose one. When Ulysses arrives disguised as a beggar, the suitors want to throw him out, but Penelope gives him hospitality. Her servant, Ulysses' old nurse, recognises him but is sworn to secrecy as he seeks revenge against the suitors who are demanding a marriage the next day. In *Act 2* Pénélope is on a hilltop seeking peace and speaks to the beggar about her husband. He proposes that a contest should be held, whoever can draw Ulysses' mighty bow and shoot an arrow through the rings of twelve axes shall have her hand. In *Act 3* the suitors fail, Ulysses succeeds, kills the suitors, and Pénélope and Ulysses are reunited in joy.

The *Prélude* is serious and grand using a large orchestra when necessary and with some shades of Wagner's *Tristan*. Fauré, like Wagner, uses leitmotivs for characters and critical objects, but unlike Wagner he sets a fast dramatic pace. *Act 1* includes every emotion, fast moving repartee with the suitors, longing memories of Ulysses for Pénélope, a joyful lovesong *Épouse chérie* for Ulysses. *Act 2* opens with a most evocative introduction of landscape and seascape, the mood peaceful. Pénélope's great duet with the disguised Ulysses is gripping with rich and detailed accompaniment. The conclusion of the act, Ulysses with the shepherds, is triumphant, with whooping horns. *Act 3's Prélude* warns of Ulysses impending revenge. There is a masterly build up to the entrance of the Queen, and Antinous – the leading suitor – is surprisingly given a lovely aria. Throughout the storm and longbow scenes Fauré provides highly original and evocative music, tension building all the time through the cymbal clashes as Ulysses reveals himself, to the death of the suitors. The conclusion is led by a passionate duet for the reunited couple that erupts into a great choral climax with a sweeping melody in a radiant C major.

Maurice Ravel

7

RAVEL

Ravel *His Life*

Maurice Ravel was born on March 7, 1875, in Ciboure, a fishing village in the Basque region of South-west France. He was the first of two sons born to Pierre-Joseph Ravel and his wife Marie, who returned to her own native village for the birth of her first child. Pierre-Joseph was Swiss, an outstanding engineer and inventor who created an early automobile. He had settled in Paris in the 1860s, met his wife in Spain and married her in 1873. Maurice's younger brother Edouard was to become a talented painter.

A few months after Maurice's birth the family was living in the artistic village of Montmartre, close to the heart of Paris. The composers Fauré and Chabrier lived close by. As the young Ravel grew up it was clear that he had a great sensitivity to music and he started piano lessons at the age of six. Ravel's childhood was happy and although he didn't attend school he received a good education, primarily from his parents. In May 1882 Ravel became a piano pupil of the composer Henry Ghys and rapidly made progress. When he was twelve he started learning music theory and composition and it was there that he found his true metier.

At the age of 13 Ravel befriended an ambitious Spanish pianist of the same age, Ricardo Viñes, and their relationship was to be enduring and stimulating. In the early days they frequently played piano duets together and experimented with new compositions. The Exposition Universelle in 1889 provided opportunities for them to experience the works of modern Russian composers conducted by Rimsky-Korsakov, as well as music played by a gamelan orchestra from South-east Asia. At this time Ravel auditioned for the Paris Conservatoire and was awarded a place in the preparatory piano class.

Ravel's career at the Conservatoire, both in piano and composition, was a chequered one. His small stature gave him hands that were not well-suited to achieving virtuoso effects on the piano. It was a time of substantial artistic development for him, however, and he read widely and developed his tastes and values. He gained a certain reputation as a dandy and always dressed immaculately and for effect. Of course life in Montmartre was exciting and over the years he got to know the composers Erik Satie and Chabrier, as well as Fauré and Debussy. The Englishman Frederick Delius and the Norwegian Edouard Grieg also influenced him.

Ravel did not make sufficient progress at the Conservatoire and he left in 1895 with a few serious compositions, songs and piano works, under his belt. The same year he completed *Habanera* (later to be orchestrated and included in the *Rhapsodie espagnole*). Changes at the Conservatoire, in particular the appointment of Gabriel Fauré as Professor of Composition, persuaded Ravel to re-apply and this time he benefited from the thorough teaching of Andre Gédalge. A violin sonata was written at this time but remained unpublished until 1975.

By 1897 Ravel was set on a career as a composer. Initially he concentrated on piano works. Debussy heard his music and was so taken by *Habanera* that he borrowed a copy of the score from Ravel. This episode has always been controversial because Debussy is reputed to have lost the score and only returned it some years later. What is known is that parts of the music appeared in his 1903 piano work *Estampes*.

Fauré did his best to promote Ravel, introducing him into the most cultured salons and soirées of Paris where the young composer would play and accompany singers. Ravel's creative energy now turned to opera and although nothing was published, he conducted his first orchestral work, the overture *Shéhérazade*, at the Société Nationale in 1899. Later that year he completed his first masterpiece, *Pavane pour une Infante défunte* which later achieved great popularity when orchestrated in 1910.

Ravel's student days came to an end in 1900 when he was thrown out of the composition class – his efforts were considered too progressive. He continued to attend Fauré's class as an observer. However he did not give up his ambition to win the Prix de Rome, the annual musical scholarship of the Conservatoire, and he competed in four out of the next five years, unfortunately to no avail.

Ravel took full advantage of contemporary Paris life which at this time was rich in culture and artistic personalities. He still lived with his parents and as Pierre-Joseph Ravel's automobile manufacturing business dictated that they moved to less desirable locations than Montmartre, periodic trips back to his birthplace provided an increasingly appealing contrast.

For a few years he was friendly with Debussy and learnt much from him, but the most congenial group of friends he found consisted of musicians, artists and writers who revelled in the name of the *"Apaches" (the Hooligans)*. *Jeux d'eau* was a large step towards Ravel finding an individual style but the *String Quartet* that followed aroused criticism because of its similarity to Debussy. Undeterred, Ravel completed the song cycle *Shéhérazade* in 1904 and felt confident in competing again for the Prix de Rome.

The decision of the judging panel to fail Ravel at the preliminary stage of the competition caused a minor scandal, but was consistent with the past history of the competition – Berlioz was regularly overlooked when his compositions were true to his natural style and only won in 1831 when he gave the panel what it wanted. Ravel's failure mattered little because he was now considered to be an exceptionally gifted composer and he was able to attract a leading publisher prepared to give him a reasonable annual retainer. This favourable change of fortune enabled him at last to buy the quality of clothes essential for his self-image.

The *Introduction and Allegro* for harp, clarinet, flute and string quartet was written quickly in 1905 to a commission from the well-known instrument firm of Erard. That summer Ravel enjoyed an extended boat trip that took him through northern France and on to Belgium, the Netherlands and Germany. The break refreshed Ravel and during the remainder of the year he completed a number of significant piano works including *Sonatine* and *Miroirs* before starting on a major operatic project *La Cloche engloutie*. Ravel was embroiled in another scandal that year as a result of the publication of *Histoires naturelles*. These were settings of some of Jules Renard's descriptions of nature and were viewed as outrageously progressive.

The health of Pierre-Joseph Ravel was failing and the composer felt he had to satisfy his father's ambition of seeing an opera by his son. Ravel stopped work on *La Cloche engloutie* and started work on *L'Heure espagnole*, a short comedy. Although published in short score in 1908 just before Joseph's death, Ravel was not able to secure its premiere until 1911.

At the beginning of 1908 Ravel took on the English composer Ralph Vaughan Williams, who was three years older than himself, as a pupil in orchestration. It was an unusual but mutually beneficial experience. During this period Ravel was orchestrating *Rhapsodie espagnole* ready for its premiere in March. Despite its modern effects it was recognised as a masterpiece and Ravel's skill in orchestration was much commented on. Next Ravel returned to the piano and *Gaspard de la nuit*, three piano pieces influenced by a collection of poems of that title.

The death of his father devastated Ravel but the family was now able to move back into the centre of Paris and Ravel could see more of his friends. He started work on *Ma Mère l'Oye (Mother Goose)*. Vaughan Williams invited him to London in April 1909 and both the composer and his music were well received. In protest at the conservative way in which the Société Nationale de Musique was being run, Ravel and several of his colleagues formed the Société Musicale Indépendant to foster performance of a wider range of music. Gabriel Fauré agreed to be its first president.

In June Ravel was surprised and delighted to receive a commission from Diaghilev of the Ballets Russes for a ballet score based on the legend of *Daphnis et Chloé*. Ravel's commission preceded that given to Stravinsky for *The Firebird* but Ravel worked slowly (and devoted time to *Ma Mère l'Oye*) and it was the Russian's work, an extraordinary success, that dominated the 1910 season. Diaghilev was content to have *Daphnis et Chloé* held over until 1912, allowing Ravel time to ensure the premiere of *L'Heure espagnole* at the Opéra Comique.

Ravel completed the score of *Daphnis et Chloé* at Ciboure during the summer of 1911 and also created an orchestral score of *Ma Mère l'Oye* as another ballet. *Daphnis et Chloé* was premiered on June 8, 1912, and caused a degree of controversy since much of the sexual content and imagery of the original text had been eliminated. However it was clearly a masterpiece and a success.

Ravel needed a long break after the tensions of bringing his ballet to fruition. The next project again stemmed from Diaghilev but this time involved working with the impresario's prime composer, Igor Stravinsky, in creating a new orchestration of Mussorgsky's unfinished opera *Khovanshchina* – Rimsky-Korsakov's earlier version being deemed unsatisfactory. The two composers knew each other well and collaborated effectively.

The next significant composition was *Trois Poèmes de Stéphane Mallarmé*. Ravel's settings of the poet were matched by Claude Debussy, another example of the two composers' paths crossing. At the end of 1913 Ravel again visited England, before he passed through Paris for an extended stay in St.Jean-de-Luz near Ciboure where the *Piano Trio* was the main outcome. The onset of the Great War was a profound shock to someone of Ravel's sensibilities and he had a strong desire to follow his brother into the army. He was rejected on account of his health but persisted and was eventually accepted into the artillery in March 1915. His real ambition, however, was to join the newly created air force as an observer.

Ravel experienced the full horrors of war, mainly as a driver supporting the front line during 1916. By 1917 he was posted to a less active area and while recuperating from dysentery he returned to Paris to find his mother close to death. She died at her home in January 1917 with both her sons at her bedside. Her death had a profound and long-lasting effect on Ravel who had doted on her and had never had any other intimate female companion. Ravel returned to his post but fell ill again and was released from the army in June.

Having lived with his parents all his life, Ravel's life was now severely disrupted. He chose to live with Mme.Fernand Dreyfus, the step-mother of one of his pupils, who had written and sent food parcels to him during Ravel's time as a soldier. She replaced his mother and he used the family homes in Paris and Rouen as he recovered and worked on completing *Le Tombeau de Couperin*. Afterwards he returned to Paris and joined his brother, who himself had moved in with friends. Paris was still under bombardment from the Germans. The Spanish flu epidemic nearly finished him and certainly left him depressed and lethargic and unable to compose for some time.

109

The death of Debussy in 1917 had pushed Ravel into the position of the leading French composer of the day and it was not long before some important commissions were proposed to him. One was for *L'Enfant et les Sortilèges* for the Opéra, and the other was a Diaghilev commission for *La Valse*, an idea that had been with Ravel for many years. To make this possible a friend lent him a house far south of Paris in the isolated Ardèche region, an ideal place for composition and recovery.

During Ravel's stay in the Ardèche he was notified that the state wished to make him a Chevalier of the Légion d'honneur. This was the last thing that Ravel wanted but before he had time to refuse he was appalled to discover the honour announced in the press. His rejection of the honour created another controversy. On his return to Paris Ravel played *La Valse* for Diaghilev and a group that included Stravinsky and Francis Poulenc, one of the brightest young French composers. Diaghilev did not find the work congenial as a ballet, calling it a *"a portrait of a ballet"*. Stravinsky did not utter a word, and Ravel was deeply offended by both of them.

Ravel at last acquired a house of his own, Le Belvédère, in the village of Montfort l'Amaury, 30 miles from Paris. It was to be his home for the rest of his life, enlarged, decorated, furnished and tailored to his needs, with everything scaled down in size for him. He was still depressed and composed little for some time, but he travelled a good deal to perform his music in Europe. Ravel also kept a room in a hotel in Paris which he often visited, frequently returning to the night-life of Montmartre.

In 1922 Ravel met Bartók who was accompanying the violinist Jelly Arányi on a European concert tour. Ravel was much taken by Jelly (as were Bartók and Elgar) and her playing of Hungarian folk music and he decided to write a concert rhapsody, *Tzigane*, for her. He was also persuaded by the Director of the Monte Carlo Opéra to complete *L'Enfant et les Sortilèges* which had a great success when it was premiered in Monte Carlo in March 1925.

Next Ravel completed his *Violin Sonata in G* which he and the composer/violinist George Enescu premiered in May 1927. The second movement, entitled *Blues*, aroused much comment. At the end of the year Ravel at last undertook the long concert tour of North America that had long been proposed to him. During a stay of several months he gave a number of recitals and conducted all the leading orchestras.

Amongst the many famous people he met was George Gershwin who played *Rhapsody in Blue* at a party to celebrate Ravel's birthday. He turned down Gershwin's request for lessons in composition, saying "*It is better to write good Gershwin than bad Ravel!*"

Financially enriched by the tour, Ravel returned to France to rest but also now with a will to compose. Before his trip he had been given a commission by a leading dancer, Ida Rubinstein, to create a ballet called *Fandango* based on Albéniz's piano work *Iberia*. Much to his annoyance Ravel found that another composer had prior rights to orchestrate the music and out of this frustration came his best known work, *Boléro*, with which he fulfilled his obligation to Ida. The work was enthusiastically received at its premiere at the Opéra in Paris in November 1928 and was to produce substantial royalties for the composer.

The idea of a further American visit was attractive to Ravel and he intended to write a piano concerto with which to tour, as Stravinsky had done some five years earlier. This was interrupted by a commission for the *Concerto for the left hand* from the pianist Paul Wittgenstein who had lost his right arm in the Great War. This was not the first time Wittgenstein was not over-impressed with the result of his commission, although he changed his mind on deeper acquaintance. But his attitude upset Ravel and discouraged him from pressing on with his own concerto and the American tour was thus shelved.

Ravel finally completed his *Concerto in G* at the end of 1931 and it was premiered by an old friend, the pianist Marguerite Long, in January of the following year, with Ravel conducting. The two undertook an extensive concert tour of Europe with the new work. Wittgenstein had also premiered the *Concerto for left hand* in Vienna in January and Ravel's tour enabled him to be at a private performance of the work at the pianist's home shortly afterwards. Ravel was appalled to discover that Wittgenstein had modified his work but was unable to stop the pianist – who had exclusive performing rights for six years – from continuing to perform the adulterated version.

Ravel's health had been giving concern for some time and the tour left him physically exhausted. He spent the summer in St.Jean-de-Luz, working on a commission for three songs that formed *Don Quichotte à Dulcinée*. It was to be his last composition. In October he was involved in a car crash that shook him badly and his ability to co-ordinate his movements and speech became increasingly impaired. There were to be periods of remission but Ravel conducted for the last time in November 1933. He was able to compose music in his head but suffered the great frustration of being unable to put pen to paper. Travel was appealing and still possible for a while but by 1936 he was largely confined to his home at Belvédère, regularly visited by friends.

Towards the end of 1937 Edouard Ravel was persuaded that a brain operation might restore his brother's faculties. As the composer was also now suffering pain it was decided to operate. Ravel went into hospital on December 17, unaware of what was planned and underwent surgery without anaesthetic. He survived the operation but quickly fell into a coma and died on December 28. Ravel was buried in a quiet ceremony two days later in the cemetery of Levallois-Perret in Paris, alongside his parents.

Ravel *The Person*

Ravel was slim and only 5ft.3ins tall. He had a mop of wavy dark hair that later turned into an elegant swept-back style, and a long aquiline nose. His shortness gave him an inferiority complex. Numerous people commented that he looked like a jockey. While not vain it was extremely important for him to be immaculately and elegantly dressed and he liked to be at the forefront of fashion.

Although he tended to keep himself aloof from others he had numerous friends. Underneath he was a sensitive and passionate person He could get very prickly with people and was easily slighted. His sexuality has been the subject of speculation but the evidence is that he largely suppressed it, finding the subject distasteful, whilst occasionally frequenting prostitutes. He loved children and he did propose to a close friend, the violinist Hélène Jourdan-Morhange but she turned him down. He was aware that marriage would create chaos in his tidy life.

Ravel was highly intelligent, extremely professional ("*tortured by the itch for perfection*" according to Léon-Paul Fargue), civilised and well read. He was modest (praise embarrassed him), moral, loyal to his friends, an egalitarian and an atheist. He could be very absent-minded.

He loved walking and travelling and in his last years his love of flowers and trees resulted in a special garden, tended by a gardener as he did not like to get his hands dirty. He loved animals, particularly cats and at Belvédère he had a family of Siamese. He smoked heavily and created his own cocktails which he delighted to serve to friends on the terrace at Belvédère in the evening. Before lunch he served Pernod. Ravel loved a night out in Paris and had a propensity for fun, enjoying pleasures with the delight of a child.

Ravel *His Music*

Ravel was a highly sensitive musician who brought a great finesse to his works. He was a brilliant orchestrator, handling all the instruments with consummate feeling for their colour and capability. An ability to conjure up images in music is always evident.

For the "Ravel Starter Pack" I propose the following works:

1 Introduction and Allegro This work is scored for harp, string quartet (or orchestra), flute and clarinet. This is Ravel at his best, beautiful chamber music or, with string orchestra like a miniature harp concerto. The mood is relaxed and evocative, the instruments meandering like a river in the height of summer.

2 Daphnis et Chloé is one of the most brilliant of all ballet scores, scored for a very large orchestra and a wordless chorus. The ancient Greek tale tells how Daphnis wins a kiss from Chloé who is then abducted by pirates. She is saved by the intervention of the great God Pan and reunited with Daphnis. For its numerous dances and romantic interludes Ravel creates glorious music, from delicate to overwhelming, from sensuous to bacchanalian, using a gloriously rich orchestral palette.

3 Piano Concerto in G This opens with a great fairground bustle. The piano's opening theme is memorably jazzy. Ravel makes the most of it and contrasts it well with contemplative passages. The conclusion is stunning, with brilliant orchestral writing. The heartfelt *adagio* has the piano unfolding a simple but beautiful theme before a flute and the orchestra join in. The conversation between the piano and the orchestra becomes more intense before the movement ends in tranquillity. The concluding *presto* is again jazz-like, with trombones sliding up and down the scale, nimble piano work and superb orchestration and fanfares. Enormous fun!

Orchestral Music

Here are some real masterpieces, let's start with the famous *Boléro* which I'm sure that you won't need me to tell you about. But it is an extraordinarily hypnotic work, a great orchestral crescendo on a simple theme that builds from next to nothing to a frightening climax. By Ravel's own admission there is a strong representation in the music of an industrial factory punching out its products.

With Ravel's Basque origins it is not surprising that the *Rhapsodie espagnole* is superbly evocative, the southern Mediterranean oozing from this collection of four pieces. *Prélude à la nuit* is mysterious, evocative, erupting into shimmering climaxes and full of anticipation. *Malagena* is strongly rhythmic, surging, and explodes into Spanish dance before vanishing. *Habanera* is restless then has hesitant strings enunciating a rhythm that never quite catches fire. *Feria* brings the work to a brilliant conclusion, where you can almost see the crowds and the dancers and smell the Spanish air.

La Mère l'Oye (Mother Goose) originated as piano pieces but Ravel produced a glorious orchestration that makes this ballet in six tableaux one of his most popular works and it's ideal for children. The *Prélude* has a wistful, dreamlike quality to it, but erupts into the heavily syncopated *Danse du Rouet*. *Pavane for Sleeping Beauty* follows, lazy woodwind in a simple and memorable melody with the string accompaniment pizzicato at first, quietly radiant later. *Beauty and the Beast* captures the two participants in marvellous representations, violins versus bassoon, with a glorious solo violin part and a ravishing close. The penultimate tableau, *Empress of the Pagodas*, bustles to the sound of flutes and oriental music, brilliantly snappy. The Beast turns into a handsome Prince in the *Fairy Garden*, where the interlude is magical, again with solo violin prominent and leading to a noble slow movement which in turn builds to a superb climax, with harps prominent.

The orchestration of *Le Tombeau de Couperin* has much appeal. The *Prélude* is fast moving and brilliant, *Forlane* is a traditional dance with a pastoral mood and *Menuet* is an elegiac movement with rich strings and a prominent oboe part. The piece concludes with *Rigaudon*, a high spirited dance with a brash opening and close.

The short *La Valse* is a Viennese waltz transferred to an orchestral canvas of infinite subtlety and exquisite colouring. More entertaining waltzes come in the *Valses nobles et sentimentales* – eight of them, varying from one to four minutes with great variations of tempo and mood. These are delightful entertainment and conclude with *Epilogue*, a wistful leave-taking.

If you have taken to the *Piano Concerto in G* then the *Piano Concerto for left hand* will not disappoint. Its highly original opening has growling basses and double bassoon through which the orchestra gradually emerges into daylight and a grand climax. Immediately this is followed by an extended piano solo, in initially sombre mood. The orchestra answers with increasing brilliance and then piano and orchestra meditate together for the first time. Ravel uses the full orchestral palette, brass and percussion to the fore. The bass drum marks the seamless switch to the second section, a jaunty march. A pizzicatto passage leads into a grandiose third section that dies away leaving the long reflective solo piano part that takes the work to the last minute when the orchestra returns with great shrieking chords – stupendous!

Piano Music

Ravel's piano music matches as far as is possible the finesse of his orchestral music and often there is the opportunity to make comparisons. For piano duet there are transcriptions of numerous works plus the original *La Mère l'Oye*. Solo piano pieces include *le Tombeau de Couperin* and *Valses nobles et sentimentales*.

His principal unique piano work is *Gaspard de la nuit*, inspired by three poems. In three movements, the outer two, *Ondine* and *Scarbo* are brilliant, particularly the latter. The central *Le gibet (the gallows)* is exceptionally haunting and evocative with a far-away bell sounding throughout the movement.

Miroirs has five pieces including the vibrant *Alborado del gracioso*, well known in its orchestral form. Each is a little gem of a picture in music, the total making a superb concert piece.

Chamber Music

Ravel's *String Quartet* is a popular masterpiece. Its opening *allegro moderato* is initially elegantly questioning, but then sets off purposefully, led by the cello. Listen for some innovative effects. After a fast and brilliant second movement with lots of pizzicato, the viola leads a profoundly moving song in the third movement *Très lent*. The final movement shatters the calm with powerful and agitated force.

Ravel's superb *Piano Trio* opens with a piano motive that Ravel described as *"basque in colour"*. The mood of the movement, marked *Modéré*, oscillates between restlessness and reflection, the music of great transparency, the close of gentle calm. *Pantoum* has complex rhythms as in the Malayan pantun verse form and makes a brilliant and original scherzo. The *Passacaille* has an expansive theme that often sings in its variations, the overall mood one of sadness. The *Finale* opens with exotic string sounds and then creates an almost orchestral sound in this brilliant movement which ends with stunning fanfares for the piano. If this were orchestrated it would be famous!

The Sonata for Violin and Piano in G is a Ravel masterpiece, notable for its absorption of 1920s jazz and dance influences, in particular for its second movement entitled *Blues*. It opens with plucked violin strings, later taken up by the piano as the violin sings – highly original. The sonata ends with a scintillating *Perpetuum mobile*, the piano spraying notes towards its brilliant conclusion. There is also an early *Violin Sonata in A minor* which was performed in public for the first time in 1975. It is an entertaining piece and bears Ravel's imprint.

Operas

Ravel wrote two exquisite little operas that make easy listening. The libretto of Ravel's opera *L'enfant et les sortilèges (The child and the spells)* was written by Colette, the famous music-hall star and author. The work is a 45-minute fairy-tale opera about a spoilt young child, bored and living in the French countryside. He is out to make mischief and when left alone he smashes a teapot, tears up his books, pulls the cat's tail and swings on the pendulum of the grandfather clock. Suddenly all the furniture comes to life and he is rebuked by all that he has destroyed, including the Princess from the fairy-tales that he has ripped up. Arithmetic makes an unforgettable appearance. The animals have their turn in the garden but the Child bandages a wounded squirrel and they relent and return the repentant child to his home. This little opera is great fun and Ravel is in his element writing brilliant and magical music. He makes sparing use of the orchestra, often using chamber music effects. The passage between the Child (sung by a soprano) and the Princess is very touching, the Child's following aria exquisite. The *Cat's duet* has miaows all round and the music of the insects is superbly evocative. And so it rushes on to a happy ending with full chorus and orchestra. It is an ideal introductory opera for children.

L'Heure Espagnol is a hilarious musical farce about hanky-panky in the shop of Torquemada, a clockmaker. His wife Concepcion is seeking some romantic fun and her lovers get ferried upstairs in the cases of grandfather clocks to avoid discovery. The *Introduction* has ticking clocks and tolling bells to set the scene. The orchestra, used sparingly, is a full one and Ravel creates a strong Spanish flavour, all the time painting musical pictures to provide a running commentary. The concluding quintet – there are only five roles – is the only ensemble and is a hilarious Spanish send-up with a hefty orchestral conclusion.

Other Music

Ravel's magical song cycle *Shéhérazade* consists of settings of three poems for soprano and orchestra. *Asie*, the first and easily the longest, is an exotic concoction, Ravel is again at his most delicate and colourful. *La flûte enchantée* is an ideal subject, flute and voice duetting, the mood languid and sensuous. The flute also opens *L'indifférent*, equal in beauty and mood.

There are also numerous songs, some of which have orchestral accompaniment.

Bartók Béla

8

BARTÓK

Bartók *His Life*

*B*éla Bartók was born on March 25, 1881, in the Hungarian town of Nagyszentmiklos, which was later ceded to Rumania. His parents, Bela and Paula, were both teachers, his father having succeeded his own father as headmaster of a local school. As they were also music-lovers the young Béla's musical education started early and his affinity for music quickly became apparent.

Bartók's father died in 1887, by which time his other child, Elza, was three. Paula Bartók was forced to return to teaching in order to support her family. Bartók's musical education was her top priority during the next six years spent on the move. Piano lessons had developed Bartók's talent sufficiently for him to appear in his first public concert in 1892, when he included one of his own compositions.

The family's wanderings finally came to an end in 1894 when Paula was appointed to a post at a teacher training college in Pozsony (now Bratislava), a substantial city with a university. At last there was some stability and Bartók's piano teachers were now of a much higher calibre. To assist his composing Bartók became an avid purchaser of orchestral scores which he studied intensely.

Four years ahead of Bartók was another music prodigy, Ernst von Dohnányi, whom he succeeded as organist at a local church. Dohnányi, after graduating from the Budapest Academy of Music (founded in 1875 with the strong support of Franz Liszt), achieved a grand success after a concerto performance in London under the conductor Hans Richter. In 1899 and with Dohnányi as a role model, Bartók chose to enroll at the Budapest Academy rather than to take up a place he had been offered at the Vienna Conservatoire.

In Bartók's first year he was dogged by illness, a portent for the rest of his life. His concerned mother demanded that he move in with one or other of his two aunts who lived locally. Bartók's principal piano teacher was István Thomán, one of many pianists who had studied with Liszt. Thomán recognised Bartók's gifts and nurtured the development of both the man and his music.

Musical and social life in Budapest were stimulating. Bartók taught numerous students including the future wife of another prodigy, Zoltán Kodály, and the elder sisters of Jelly Aranyi who was destined to become a famous international violin soloist. Bartók developed a romantic attachment with a fellow student.

It took Richard Strauss, the most celebrated living composer of the time, to re-ignite Bartók's interest in composing. A performance of the tone poem *Also Sprach Zarathustra* in 1902 provided the spark and Bartók soon made a piano transcription of Strauss's *Ein Heldenleben* which he performed at the Tonkünstlerverein in Vienna. To coincide with a resurgence of nationalism in Hungary Bartók composed a tone poem of his own, named after *Kossuth*, the hero of the 1848 uprising. *Kossuth* was premiered in Budapest in 1904 and put Bartók's name on the musical map in his homeland. A month later he travelled to England and heard Hans Richter perform the work in a concert with the Hallé Orchestra in which Bartók was also a soloist.

Bartók's composing took a new, and more dominant, direction as the result of a chance meeting. Bartók had taken himself off to the countryside to compose and practice and there he heard his neighbours' maid singing a Hungarian folksong. Intrigued by the song, Bartók was introduced to a rich vein of true national culture and history that was to be a profound influence.

Life for the struggling pianist/composer was hardly easy. When Bartók entered the Rubinstein Competition in Paris he failed to win either the piano or composition prizes. This was deflating for Bartók's ego, and he was forced to think seriously of how he could earn an income.

A new and ultimately lifelong relationship started in 1906 when Bartók met Zoltán Kodály, a fellow student at the Budapest Academy. Kodály was well educated and had a Ph.D. based on research into Hungarian folk music. The two were to share their interests and efforts in this field.

Bartók's financial circumstances took a turn for the better in 1907 when he was appointed Professor at the Academy, teaching piano. Kodály had earlier been appointed Professor of Composition. Bartók's new role gave him the opportunity to devote time to folksongs. The new technology of recording also enabled him to make valuable field expeditions, and he would go off into the Hungarian countryside armed with a gramophone and wax cylinders. Like other composers such as Vaughan Williams in England and Janáček in Moravia he was genuinely concerned that the heritage of traditional folk music might be lost in the industrialised age.

The same year Bartók met and fell in love with Stefi Geyer, a violin student at the Academy. He shared his most intimate thoughts with her, often in letters. Although unfortunately his feelings were not reciprocated, she is immortalised in the dedication of the *Violin Concerto No. 1*. Bartók suppressed the work, and it was not published or premiered until after Stefi's death in 1956. When Stefi ended the relationship Bartók was devastated but threw his energies into composing the *String Quartet No. 1*, the first of a famous series of six, as well as a number of piano pieces where he worked off his anger and frustration.

Some months later he took on the 15-year-old Márta Ziegler as a piano player. One November morning in 1909 Bartók gave her a piano lesson and after lunch they left the house, but returned later to continue the lesson. In the evening Bartók announced to his mother that Márta would be staying for dinner as they had just got married.

In December 1909 the newly-weds visited Paris for a stay of several months but little was achieved. Later, in Zurich, Bartók developed a brief friendship with the English composer Frederick Delius. His main artistic ambition at this time was to win a competition to compose an opera. Bartók had been enthused by Béla Balázs' libretto of *Duke Bluebeard's Castle* and he set to work composing the score, his first masterpiece although it failed to win the prize. A son, also named Béla, was born in September 1911, the month the score was finished. Field trips to Scandinavia and Scandinavia provided further variety in Bartók's routines.

A visit to Budapest in 1913 by Diaghilev's *Ballets Russes* resulted indirectly in the Opera House giving Bartók a ballet commission, but the next year Europe was thrown into a state of war. Bartók applied for military service but was turned down because of the poor state of his health. He was thus able to spend the war years carrying out field research. Whilst doing this he met Klára Gombussy, a 15-year-old with a penchant for writing poetry. Undoubtedly smitten, Bartók set several of her poems to music. In 1916 he started work on the ballet score *The Wooden Prince* with a libretto by Balázs, completing it in the following year. Its premiere in Budapest was a great success and the composer completed *String Quartet No.2* in the same year, in his now recognizable style.

Bartók's musical research provided the basis for a concert of traditional soldiers' songs that was given in Vienna in January 1918 for an establishment audience. Bartók accompanied and gained valuable exposure that resulted in an approach from one of the leading music publishers, Universal Edition who were to publish his works for the next 20 years. Soon afterwards several of Bartók's works were premiered in Budapest, most importantly *Duke Bluebeard's Castle*. Because it was a relatively short work it was partnered by the ballet *The Wooden Prince*.

In the summer of 1918 Bartók was working on his next stage work, *The Miraculous Mandarin*, and undertaking his last recording trips into the countryside, when the frightening Spanish flu epidemic nearly killed him. The Austrian Empire fragmented at the end of the Great War, and Hungary's boundaries shrank as parts seceded or were absorbed by neighbouring countries. Communism, extending beyond its initial success in Russia, had become a powerful force and in March 1919 it was the communists who led the Councils of the new Hungarian Republic.

Bartók was expected to become a member, along with Kodály and Dóhnanyi, of the newly launched Directorate of Music, but control by the state was not to his taste. These were traumatic times and the Rumanian Army, which had earlier occupied part of Hungary, was allowed into Budapest as the communists fled. Bartók's house was one of many they commandeered. Political events resolved themselves in 1920 with the appointment of a regent, Count Miklós.

Being a composer in these circumstances was not easy but Bartók strengthened his links with the outside world by undertaking musical projects in other countries, including America and England. Out of the blue Jelly Arányi visited Bartók in 1921. She and her sisters had been trapped in England at the outbreak of the Great War and she was now a famous international violin virtuoso. Bartók agreed to compose a violin sonata for her and also to accompany her on a concert tour, principally in England but also including Paris where he met all the leading French composers plus Stravinsky. A second violin sonata was written for Jelly in 1922 but touring soured their relationship – probably Bartók made an unwanted pass at her.

Bartók's marriage had survived many crises but in 1923 he started an affair with Ditta Pásztory, a very attractive 20-year-old student of his at the Budapest Academy. At first Márta Bartók seemed to take the situation dispassionately but after quietly confronting him she asked for a divorce. This was arranged extremely quickly and by the end of August Bartók was married to Ditta.

Inspired by his new love and the birth of a second son, Peter, Bartók entered into a prolific period in which he concentrated on the piano. Like Stravinsky he realised that there was a good demand for composer-pianists and he was able to attract profitable engagements. He undertook an extensive tour of America starting in December 1926 and followed it up with a major tour of Europe.

By 1930, with the *Third* and *Fourth String Quartets* completed and launched, Bartók now entered his final period as a composer. Known, respected, but not popular, he still needed to teach. His work as a composer retained a Hungarian perspective, the *Cantata Profane* being a prime example. Meanwhile the political forces at work in neighbouring Germany also influenced life in Hungary and created an increasingly unattractive environment in which to live and work.

Bartók moved out of Budapest in 1932 and resigned from the Academy of Music in 1934, joining instead the Hungarian Academy of Sciences where he could concentrate on folk music. Commissions arrived for the *Fifth String Quartet* and the *Music for Strings, Percussion and Celesta*, the latter quickly achieving international exposure. *Makrokosmos* was written as a piano teaching piece for his young son.

By 1938 Nazism was encroaching and Bartók switched publishers, joining Boosey & Hawkes in London. He decided to send all his important manuscripts out of Hungary. Whilst awaiting the inevitable war as Hungary aligned itself with Nazi Germany, Bartók wrote two important works, the *Divertimento for String Orchestra* and the *Sixth String*

Quartet, the latter written in August 1939. On the outbreak of war Bartók returned to Budapest but the death of his mother at the end of the year shattered him and he decided to emigrate.

In April 1940 Bartók set off alone to America for another extensive tour and also to prepare the ground for the arrival of his family. He returned to give a farewell concert in Budapest in October 1940, where Ditta made her debut and they played Mozart's *Concerto for two pianos* together. Within a week the family was on its way to America. They crossed Europe, embarked at Lisbon, and eventually arrived in New York in November. The University of Columbia immediately honoured Bartók with a doctorate and a position as a research fellow.

Like many other musical exiles from Europe, Bartók did not find life in America easy. His music was considered unappealing for the symphony audiences and of course there was a wide cultural divide. Bartók had some sponsors but the first two years were creatively barren and, more significantly, undiagnosed leukemia was taking its toll on his health. He gave his last public concert in 1942.

Bartók's tenure at Columbia ceased in the same year but Harvard University invited him to give a series of lectures. The strain of preparing and delivering these talks contributed to a collapse and a period in hospital. Whilst there he was visited by Serge Koussevitsky, the respected conductor of the Boston Symphony Orchestra. Kossevitsky regularly commissioned works from the leading composers of the day and he asked Bartók for a work for his orchestra. Thus was conceived Bartók's most popular work the *Concerto for Orchestra* on which he worked whilst he was recuperating.

In December 1943 Bartók was visited in New York by the young virtuoso Yehudi Menuhin. The meeting resulted in another commission, this time for a sonata for solo violin which was premiered the following November. The following month the *Concerto for Orchestra* gave Bartók his greatest success of all. In spite of, or perhaps because of, his illness Bartók's creativity was flourishing, and he began the *Third Piano Concerto* and the *Viola Concerto*. But at home his beloved Hungary had become a battleground for the Germans and Russians with death and destruction everywhere.

Bartók became an American citizen in 1945. In September he had a major relapse and was taken into hospital in New York, where he died on Wednesday September 26 with his wife and elder son at his bedside. The funeral took place two days later. His remains were returned to Budapest in 1988.

Bartók *The Person*

Bartók was short with a slight and delicate body. He became increasingly frail over time, his hair whitening and receding. People spoke of his piercing eyes. His health was poor throughout his life and a constant source of worry to him. He was shy and this, together with his lack of social graces, resulted in a somewhat awkward stage presence as a soloist.

A very private and secretive person, Bartók was hard-working and honest, without a natural sense of humour – laughing was not an easy response. He was unchanged by his success. He was serious, frivolity was hardly in his repertoire, and he could be prickly. He could be somewhat puritanical about material things and he didn't always show gratitude for others' efforts on his behalf, often being too engrossed with his own concerns.

Music was inevitably the most important part of his life and pupils spoke of his immaculate musicianship. They also spoke well of him and his supportive, kindly approach. When teaching he was a disciplinarian in his attitude to technique but allowed himself greater license when composing and performing.

Despite his puritanism he retained a penchant for young, vivacious women throughout much of his adult life. In his relations with them he could be immature and he offended more than one of his female musical colleagues with unwanted approaches.

He was a conservative and a traditionalist, and the state of his country was of great importance to him. He loved nature and was happiest when in the countryside. He had strong principles and was a thinker. He believed in the brotherhood of peoples and found Hungary's support of Nazi Germany in the 1930s unacceptable. His concern for humanity extended to all living things – he would not allow the family chickens to be killed during the Great War, and spent significant periods of his life as a vegetarian.

Bartók *His Music*

Bartók is one of the great composers of the twentieth century who reaches, and sometimes goes beyond, the limits of what is easily acceptable in classical music for the vast majority of listeners. This is one reason why he is so important. A voyage of discovery with Bartók's music will undoubtedly broaden the musical horizons of those prepared to make the effort.

His is a unique language and the *String Quartets*, for example, occupy a similar position in the chamber music repertoire today to the one enjoyed by Beethoven's *Late Quartets* in the past.

Here then is a carefully chosen "Bartók Starter Pack", guaranteed not to scare you away, but rather to lead you into the composer's music:

1 Concerto for Orchestra The opening declares a masterpiece, such is Bartók's command of the orchestra and the originality of the content. It has five movements, the hushed *introduzione* evolving from growling cellos and basses through skeletal violins and fluttering woodwind into a kaleidoscope of declamation and dance. The second movement is a delight, pairs of instruments taking their turns in a delicate and merry round. The outstanding *elegia* is ghostly and anguished in turn until the final bars. Its seriousness is balanced by the following *intermezzo interroto*, whose playful opening gives way to a glorious melody. All sorts of fun and games then erupt, including raspberries from the brass, and we are in the fairground for a brief spell. The brilliant *finale* is an orchestral tour-de-force, "*life-asserting*" in Bartók's own words.

2 Bluebeard's Castle In this short opera Judith, Duke Bluebeard's latest wife questions him - to his sadness - about his past. It is a symbolic work and each part of his life history is in his gloomy castle behind a bolted door, seven in all. Judith insists on his opening each door in turn, disclosing a torture chamber (make of it what you will), an armoury, riches (Judith has a sublime part here), a secret garden and behind the fifth door his dazzling kingdom. The music that accompanies the opening of the fifth door is awe-inspiring, truly sensational, as the orchestra erupts in a glorious major key chorale. After the sixth door, with its lake of tears, is the fateful seventh door, from which come Bluebeard's three former wives, all beautiful. The doubting Judith joins them when they return behind the door and the castle is plunged into darkness. The drama is intense in the hour-long work, the music superb throughout.

3 The Wooden Prince is a dance-pantomime, a fairy-tale set to seven dances between a *prélude* and a *postlude*. The music is as approachable as anything Bartók wrote, a vibrant romantic score with full orchestra. The score has been described as *"Bartók with added sugar"*! The dances are evocative with titles such as *Dance of the Princess in the Forest (Dance 1)*; *Dance of the Trees (Dance 2)*; *Dance of the Waves (Dance 3)*; *Dance of the Princess with the Wooden Doll (Dance 4)*. Overall it is most enjoyable and an easy way into the composer's work.

Orchestral

Next try the *Music for Strings, Percussion and Celesta*, which is a symphonic work of great power. In four movements, it opens mysteriously, advancing with ever increasing richness whilst eschewing seductive melodies. It is stark, and modern. The introspective passages in the first movement have a hypnotic effect. The following movement, essentially a scherzo, is lively and dance-like, highly rhythmic with the strings producing stretched sounds and the piano playing an important part. The pizzicato section is memorable. Next comes the extraordinary slow movement where Bartók creates spectacular effects – it opens with a solo xylophone, before a timpani leads to violas. The concluding movement rushes along feverishly with a sense of great fun! This is the best of "modern music"!

The *Miraculous Mandarin* is a one-act ballet about a Mandarin who has magical powers but whose mood swings between total lack of emotion and intense passion. A girl lures him into a trap where he is robbed and stabbed but will not die. Only when the girl takes him in her arms does he bleed and die. Bartók's music is a match for such a macabre plot. At times it is at the extremes of dissonance and noise, particularly in the opening which depicts a busy modern street.

Although it is brilliant it is not to everyone's taste and is perhaps best seen at the ballet. Otherwise the *Suite* from the ballet is the best way to hear the music.

The *Dance Suite* brings together several different musical cultures in a vibrant six movement structure. The dances are highly rhythmic with some great tunes. *Nos.2* and *3* are fierce Hungarian dances, *No.5* is Oriental and much slower. The *Suite* ends with brilliant brass dominant and chanting at intervals before the music dashes for the finishing line.

Two Pictures consists of *In Full Flower* and *The Village Dance*. The first is unusually expressive and romantic for Bartók, though it does have its dissonances. It certainly blossoms, ending with a magical combination of flute and harp. *Village Dance* is highly vibrant folk music, orchestra in full flow at the beginning and end, thrilling when it moves into the major key.

The *Divertimento for String Orchestra* lasts half an hour and combines grace with power. Solo instruments are prominent throughout. The opening *allegro non troppo*, whilst modern/progressive, has much that is very appealing. The *molto adagio* opens in hushed tones but grows passionate without losing intimacy before dying away – it is a lovely movement. The rhythmic string effects of the concluding *allegro assai* are great fun, but with a glorious orchestral richness throughout – and the fiery ending really brings the house down!

Concertos

The *Violin Concerto No.1* was premiered in 1956. It is one of Bartók's most romantic works, consisting of an *andante* and an *allegro giocoso*. The *andante* is an exquisite and intense meditation on Bartók's motif for Stefi Geyer, and the *allegro* is auto-biographical (and indulgent in part), miles away from the stringency of Bartók's later compositions.

Violin Concerto No.2 is substantial and sophisticated in structure, but the violin maintains sweetness in the face of a sometimes acerbic orchestra. The opening movement seems to meander initially, such is the variety of moods and tempo. The *andante tranquillo* middle movement is intense and lyrical with the exception of the middle section. An *allegro molto* leads to a fast-moving and brilliant conclusion.

Bartók's piano concertos were written in his maturity and of course he was an excellent pianist. The composer had some words to say about his *Piano Concerto No. 1* – *"its writing is a bit difficult – one might even say very difficult! – as much for orchestra as for audience."* In this exciting concerto, the *andante* offers, as so often in Bartók, an exceptional experience, this time ethereal with a celestial tread. The concluding movement *allegro: allegro molto*, is thrilling and powerful.

The composer described *"the rather light and popular character of most of the themes"* of *Piano Concerto No. 2*, and this works to the listener's advantage. It adopts Bartók's favoured, fast–slow–faster three-movement structure and there are plenty of fireworks and thrilling sounds. But the heart is the *adagio-presto-adagio* middle movement, an intense meditation where a hushed chorale from the strings converses with the piano and timpani, interrupted in the middle, in typical Bartók fashion, by a rampant *scherzo*. Hang on to your hat for the finale!

Piano Concerto No. 3 is the most accessible of the series, where you will find much melody and a great rolling theme at the heart of the first movement. The highlight is the central *adagio religioso*, its first part refering directly to Beethoven's great *adagio* in his *A minor String Quartet*. It is a gorgeous movement, its central *scherzo* full of bird-call allusions, the concluding *adagio* switching its allegiance to Bach. The *finale* is great fun, tunes and vitality build up to a virtuosic end.

Chamber Music

Bartók's *String Quartets*, along with those of Shostakovich, are renowned as the masterpieces of this genre in the 20th Century. Bartók concentrates on rhythmic variations, musical effects and thematic transformations and structure. They need patience and familiarity and their increasingly progressive idiom will not be to everyone's taste compared with the quartets of Haydn, Mozart, Beethoven and Schubert!

They are, I suggest, best approached in the order *1,2,5,6,3,4,* leaving the least approachable to the last. *No. 1* starts off with a slow, quiet and lyrical movement, the mood one of sadness. Next, after a quiet bridging passage, comes a gently rocking *allegretto* which is developed forcefully. Another bridge passage leads to a closely argued *allegro vivace*, serious stuff in the main, each instrument an equal. At the heart lies a deliciously contrasting fugue.

String Quartet No.2 opens with a *moderato* movement of gentle tempo and frequent rich sonorities. Next comes an *allegro molto capriccioso* with fierce rhythms and much invention and variety. The concluding *lento* is truly bleak and gripping.

String Quartet No.5 is a much more accessible work, in five movements, an urgent *allegro*; an absorbing *adagio molto* of great delicacy and spectral effects; a *scherzo alla bulgarese* in complex rhythms with an extraordinary trio like buzzing wasps; a static *andante*, with strange pizzicato effects, and a dance-like *finale* incorporating a whizzing fugue. Just before the end you will hear a bizarre barrel-organ-like melody.

String Quartet No.6 has four movements, each with a slow introduction. It opens with a melancholy solo viola that leads into a thoughtful vivace. The second movement leads into a distorted march with a parody of gypsy music at its centre. Next comes a *burletta* with marvellously weird sounds whose central section is almost conventionally beautiful and the quartet finishes with an extended slow movement of profound and sad mood.

String Quartet No.3 is the most dissonant quartet and the shortest. It consists of one movement in four complex sections. It has some strange sounds and some delightful effects both gentle and fiery. Try it to see if it appeals.

String Quartet No.4 has five movements, the outer ones are fast, energetic and thematically related, the second and fourth fast-moving *scherzos*, and the central movement slow. Bartók is almost in his most progressive mood but the sequence works well and each movement is highly individual. The slow movement is spare and particularly gripping – it has a passage of Bartók's *"night music"* at its own centre – and the last movement is a tour-de-force.

Violin Sonata No.1 opens with an uncompromisingly modern movement, dissonant, powerful. The *adagio* has much solo work for the violinist in its heart-searching, and the effect when the piano chords enter is magical. The exciting concluding *allegro* is like an energetic Hungarian peasant dance.

Violin Sonata No.2 has only two movements, the first opening with the violin rhapsodising, the second with pizzicato prominent. The drive of the first continues for much of the second, but it gradually vanishes into nothing.

The *Sonata for 2 pianos and percussion* is formidable. It opens pensively, with outbursts of percussion, swiftly moving into an almost orchestral *allegro molto*, with rampant percussion. The second theme is a sleeper, quiet but potentially energetic. The pent-up energy wins and the movement concludes in a storm. The *lento* is nocturnal, reminiscent of a battlefield with eerie drums. The concluding *allegro ma non troppo* is vital and enthralling as it drives towards its ebbing conclusion.

The *Sonata for Solo Violin* is a profound piece for performer and listener alike. Nearly 30 minutes long, it is a tour-de-force for the soloist in four movements, *tempo di ciaccona, fuga, melodia, presto* – the appealing *melodia* offers the easiest access point.

Bartók's *44 duos for two Violins*, each lasting about a minute, are thoroughly enjoyable pieces, based on folk-music themes. They come in eleven books of increasing difficulty and include *Cradle Song, Pillow Dance*, and conclude with a *Pizzicato* and a vital *Transylvanian Dance*.

Contrasts was commissioned by the clarinettist Benny Goodman and is scored for that instrument, plus violin and piano. Most of the interplay is between the clarinet and violin in the three movements, all of which are based on Hungarian dance. There is an attractive clarinet cadenza in the opening *Verbunkos* movement, the slow middle movement is called *Relaxation*, and in the concluding fast *Sebes* the violin is tuned for a special effect.

Piano Music

Bartók's piano music is extensive and the emphasis is on short, brilliant pieces, often with a strong folk flavour. Try *For Children* to start with and the *14 Bagatelles*. The *Folk Tunes* and *Dances (Hungarian, Rumanian, Bulgarian)* are enormous fun but for something serious try the *2 Elegies*. Bartók wrote a major set of progressive pieces for pianists (153 in total), *Mikrokosmos*, overpowering in their totality but fine in small doses.

9

BRITTEN

Britten *His Life*

*E*dward Benjamin Britten was born on St.Cecilia's Day, November 22, 1913, in Lowestoft, a fishing port in the county of Suffolk, England. His father, Robert Britten, was a dentist and his mother Edith was a keen amateur singer. Benjamin was the youngest of four children, two boys and two daughters in all.

Benjamin's mother was highly ambitious and wished her younger son to be a musician. She was deeply involved in the local choral society and visiting soloists regularly stayed with the Britten household. Edith gave her precocious son piano lessons from the age of five and he immediately showed his creative nature by composing his own music. After further piano lessons at school he was soon able to accompany his mother in her song recitals and he soon settled into a routine of getting up early each morning to compose before setting off to school.

Britten's formal education followed a traditional middle class pattern, private education at a preparatory school (where he ended up as head boy) followed by public school. He was a good and intelligent pupil and interested in sport, particularly cricket and tennis. Apart from composing and playing the piano, he added playing the viola to his accomplishments. The most formative event in those early years was his discovery of the music of Frank Bridge. Britten had first heard Bridge's music at the Norwich Festival of 1924 and he had been bowled over by it.

After Britten heard another Bridge composition at the 1927 Norwich Festival, his viola teacher introduced him to the composer. Bridge invited Britten to show him his work and thus started a teacher/pupil relationship that was to benefit Britten enormously. He visited regularly for lessons and often stayed with Bridge in the holidays.

Britten later described what Bridge gave him: *"This was immensely serious and professional study, and the lessons were mammoth.... Often I used*

to end these marathons in tears, not that he was beastly to me but the concen-
trated strain was too much for me…. In everything he did for me, there were
perhaps two cardinal principles. One was that you should try to find yourself and
be true to what you found…. The other – obviously connected with it – was his
scrupulous attention to good technique, the business of saying clearly what was in
one's mind. He gave me a sense of technical ambition."

Bridge was an important mentor who exposed Britten to the real
artistic world. He encouraged Britten to think for himself although he
inevitably had an important influence. Inevitably Bridge and Britten
debated Bridge's pacifism. When Britten wrote an essay on animals in
his last term at South Lodge he received, uniquely, no marks because of
the essay's anti-hunting sentiments. Britten's next school was Gresham's
in Norfolk. It was, in the main, an enlightened school and Britten was
highly active in the music department where some of his works were
performed.

Britten was at Gresham's for only two years before he won a scholarship to the Royal College of Music in London in 1930. Vaughan
Williams was one of the adjudicators at the entrance interview and he
later recalled that Britten arrived with a large bundle of manuscripts
under his arm. "*Is that all?*" asked Vaughan Williams and, taking him seriously, Britten responded that he had two full suitcases outside!

Initially Britten lived in lodgings close to the College but eventually
he moved in with his sister Beth in the nearby Cromwell Road. He had
only two official lessons a week at the College and he continued his
relationship with Bridge, who introduced him to modern composers,
including Mahler. This was a revelation for Britten. Britten was not
impressed with his tuition at the RCM, as, thanks to his tutor and
mentor Frank Bridge, he found himself well in advance of his contemporaries.

Amazingly, only one of his works, the *Sinfonietta, Op. 1*, was performed
at the RCM during his time there. Luckily there were enough friends
and connoisseurs to ensure that his music was performed outside the
college. In his last year he won a scholarship but when he proposed that
he should study with the avant-garde Viennese composer Alban Berg in
Vienna both the RCM and his parents deemed the idea to be inappropriate. Bridge introduced Britten to Schoenberg during the interval of
a concert at the Queen's Hall in February 1933.

A *Simple Symphony* for string orchestra was written in the winter of 1933/4 and performed at the Norwich Festival in March. A month later the *Phantasy Quartet* was performed at the International Society for Contemporary Music in Florence, but Britten was forced to return to England on hearing that his father was seriously ill. Robert Britten died before his son could reach home and the young composer spent the rest of the summer in Lowestoft, although he spent some time in London when the BBC broadcast the *Sinfonietta*.

Britten's scholarship money was used for a two month European tour in the autumn, accompanied by his mother. Their ultimate destination was Vienna where they heard many of Wagner's operas before they returned, flying from Paris on Imperial Airways. On his return Britten lived in London with Beth and started his career as a professional composer. An ideal opportunity arose when the GPO (General Post Office) Film Unit asked him to provide music for some of their documentaries such as *Night Mail*. Britten joined the staff in March 1936 with a wage of £5 per week. He also met the poet Wystan Hugh Auden and they worked on a number of projects together, forming a close friendship. This type of work required the ability to compose quickly and to deadlines, which was an invaluable experience..

Auden, who was six years older than Britten and also homosexual, had a profound influence on the young Britten. Auden was part of a vociferous circle of talented young left-wing artists living in London at a time when Europe was increasingly threatened by the rise of Nazi Germany. Through Auden Britten became Music Director of the Group Theatre where he composed incidental music for a number of plays. But most importantly he was taken on by the publisher, Boosey and Hawkes.

Life was hectic for Britten. His *Suite, Op. 6* was played at the ISCM festival in Barcelona and he composed *Our Hunting Fathers* for the Norwich Festival, set to a text by Auden. He also made his first acquaintance with the music of the Russian composer Shostakovich who impressed him deeply.

Edith Britten died in January 1937 and Auden left London in the same month to drive an ambulance in the Spanish Civil War. Two months later Britten met the man who was to be his life-long companion, the tenor Peter Pears. In May Britten was asked by Boyd Neel to

135

write a work for his string orchestra to perform at the 1937 Salzburg Festival and the *Variations on a Theme of Frank Bridge* was the result. Britten was still close to Bridge and would often discuss his compositions with him before publication.

Britten bought The Old Mill in Snape, Suffolk, in the same year and moved to live there the following Spring. There the *Piano Concerto* was written and Britten played it for the American composer Aaron Copland when he visited. Britten, an exceptional pianist, premiered it at a Queen's Hall Promenade Concert in August under Sir Henry Wood.

The Ballad of Heroes, Op.14, with part of the text written by Auden, was written in memory of Britons killed fighting for the International Brigade in the Spanish Civil War. By the time the work was premiered in April 1939 the poet had left to settle in the United States and, with Europe sliding towards war, the pacifist Britten, together with Pears, decided to follow him. After a few weeks in Canada the pair arrived in New York in June.

The New York Philharmonic performed the *Variations on a Theme of Frank Bridge* in August. Britten and Pears stayed on Long Island with the Mayers, friends of Pears. Mrs. Mayer was a serious supporter of the arts and artists and took Britten under her wing. On the declaration of war in September Britten resolved to remain in America until it was over. Early products of the stay were the *Violin Concerto* and, more importantly, the song cycle, *Les Illuminations*. Britten also joined the select group of composers who wrote a piece for the one-armed pianist, Paul Wittgenstein, *Diversions, Op.21*. The *Sinfonia da Requiem* was commissioned for Japan's celebrations of the 2,600th anniversary of the Mikado's dynasty but was rejected because of its Christian content.

In August 1940 Britten and Auden agreed a number of collaborations including an American folk-opera, *Paul Bunyan*. More immediately Britten finished the *Seven Sonnets of Michelangelo, Op.22*, the first work he wrote specifically for Pears and his distinctive tenor voice. In November Britten and Pears moved in with Auden in New York, where as usual the poet mixed with a stimulating artistic circle. But news arrived in January that Frank Bridge had died.

Paul Bunyan ran for a week in New York in May but was withdrawn after failing to create interest. Tiring of living with Auden, Britten and Pears left to stay with friends in Escondido in California. It was there

136

that Britten discovered the poetry of George Crabbe, who hailed from Aldeburgh in Suffolk, and his tale of *Peter Grimes*. Discovering Crabbe had a profound effect on Britten and he decided to return to Suffolk at the earliest opportunity.

Meanwhile the *Sinfonia da Requiem* was performed in January 1942 by the Boston Symphony Orchestra under Koussevitsky. The conductor suggested the commissioning of an opera and this was made possible with a grant from Koussevitzky's Music Foundation. Later that month Wittgenstein premiered *Diversions* with the Philadelphia Orchestra under Eugene Ormandy. In March Britten was able to book passage on a Swedish ship sailing for Liverpool and he and Pears returned home. On the voyage Britten composed *A Ceremony of Carols* and the *Hymn to St. Cecilia*, which was his last collaboration with Auden.

Soon after arriving home Britten and Pears had to appear before a tribunal as conscientious objectors. They were given exemption from call-up into the armed forces provided they gave concerts on behalf of the Council for the Encouragement of Music and the Arts. Their main base, Snape, was still occupied by Britten's sister Beth and her children. The *Sinfonia da Requiem* was performed at the Promenade Concerts in July and a number of Britten's recent works were given before the year was out. Britten met the brilliant young horn player, Dennis Brain, and composed the *Serenade for Tenor, Horn and Strings* for him.

For the tenth anniversary of the Boyd Neel Orchestra in 1943 Britten wrote the *Prelude and Fugue*. He met the composer Michael Tippett for the first time and thus began a long friendship. Tippett, who was also a homosexual and a conscientious objector, was jailed for refusing to work on a farm and in sympathy Britten and Pears gave a concert in Wormwood Scrubs jail.

Once Britten had found a librettist he started serious work on his opera *Peter Grimes* which dominated his time during 1944. It was scheduled for the eventual re-opening of the Sadler's Wells Theatre in London after the war and the premiere took place in June 1945. Peter Grimes was a great success for Britten and the first English opera to achieve a place in the international repertoire.

Immediately after the war Britten accompanied the violinist Yehudi Menuhin on a concert tour of the recently discovered German concentration camps including Belsen. Inevitably the visit had a profound effect on the pacifist composer, who wrote *The Holy Sonnets of John Donne* on his return. In November 1945, Britten, a great admirer of Henry Purcell, contributed to the celebrations for the 250th anniversary of the composer's death. He used a theme of Purcell's as the basis for a commission from the Ministry of Education for a work to demonstrate the different instruments of the orchestra in a film. Thus was born the work usually known as *The Young Person's Guide to the Orchestra*.

Britten visited Tanglewood in the United States in August 1946 for the American premiere of *Peter Grimes* conducted by Leonard Bernstein. Opera politics in England led Britten and his circle to try to set up a new touring company and a chamber opera, *The Rape of Lucretia*, was written with this in mind. An initial collaboration with Glyndebourne Opera introduced *The Rape of Lucretia* to English audiences in 1946, but it had a poor reception. In the following year the English Opera Group was founded. Britten was one of the artistic directors and he wrote *Albert Herring* for the 1947 season. It was premiered by the English Opera Group at Glyndebourne and they later toured it in Holland and Switzerland.

In 1947 Britten and Pears moved from the Old Mill House to Crag House in Aldeburgh and soon afterwards Pears proposed that they create a music festival there. They were able to raise funding and the first Aldeburgh Festival took place in June 1948. It included *Albert Herring* and the new cantata *St. Nicholas*. The overall success of the Festival determined Britten to make it an annual event. It became the focus for Britten's work and gradually developed over the years into a music festival of the highest stature, attracting many famous artists and composers.

1949 saw the composition of the *Spring Symphony* for Koussevitsky and *Let's Make an Opera!* for Aldeburgh. Britten started work on another major opera, *Billy Budd*, with Eric Crozier and the writer E.M.Forster as librettists. *Billy Budd* was premiered at Covent Garden in December 1951 to mixed reviews. Such was Britten's fame by now that 1952 saw the publication of *Benjamin Britten: a commentary on his works by a group of specialists*. This formidable publication aroused a fair deal of criticism in the music establishment because of its sycophancy and Britten, who despised critics and did not like criticism, found himself at the centre of the controversy.

The imminent coronation of Queen Elizabeth II in 1953 resulted in the commission of another opera, *Gloriana*, about the first Queen Elizabeth. It was premiered at Covent Garden six days after the coronation and was not well-received. Britten was made a Companion of Honour, but the opera quickly vanished from performance. Undeterred, Britten accepted a commission for the Venice Festival and the resulting opera, *The Turn of the Screw*, was premiered at La Fenice in September 1954.

A visit to Bali in 1956 allowed Britten to experience the gamelan orchestra, some of whose musical effects were incorporated in *The Prince of the Pagodas*, a ballet score premiered on the first day of 1957. Later that year he moved from his sea-front home to the Red House, situated in a quieter part of Aldeburgh. There he completed *Noye's Fludde* which was first performed at the 1958 Aldeburgh Festival. The *Nocturne* quickly followed.

For the 1960 Aldeburgh Festival Britten chose *A Midsummer Night's Dream* with Shakespeare's text modified by Britten and Pears. It proved a considerable success and was taken up by a number of international opera houses. In September Britten met Shostakovich when the Russian composer came for the London premiere of his *Cello Concerto No.1*. Afterwards Shostakovich introduced Britten to the soloist, Mstislav Rostropovich, and thus started a unique artistic friendship between the cellist and the English composer.

Rostropovich asked Britten to compose a cello sonata that was completed five months later. Rostropovich and his wife, the soprano Galina Vishneskaya, stayed with Britten for the 1961 Aldeburgh Festival when the cellist and composer performed the work together. The next project was a major choral work commissioned for the dedication of the rebuilt Coventry Cathedral which replaced the one destroyed in the Second World War. The idea appealed strongly to the pacifist Britten and he created a highly original work, combining a traditional requiem mass with more intimate settings of poems by the poet Wilfred Owen, himself killed in the First World War.

For the premiere Britten wanted the three soloists to be of English, Russian and German nationalities but politics prevented Galina Vishnevskaya from participating. The premiere took place in May 1962 and the *War Requiem* made a profound impact with its denunciation of war and its message of reconciliation. It was the pinnacle of Britten's career. Its impact, rare for a premiere, was felt internationally and when the recording company Decca released the work a year later it sold an unprecedented 200,000 copies in just a few months.

Britten and Pears visited the Soviet Union in March 1963 for a festival of British music and spent time with both Shostakovich and Rostropovich. For the latter he composed the *Cello Symphony*. Back in England his 50th birthday was celebrated with numerous performances of his music including a rare concert performance of *Gloriana*. The following year he wrote *Curlew River,* the first of a number of parables for church performance. These were mini-operas based on an ancient form of Japanese play that Britten had seen in Tokyo some years earlier. It was premiered along with the *Cello Symphony* at that year's Aldeburgh Festival.

Britten's celebrity status was demonstrated when he received the first Aspen Award in the Humanities in July 1964. The award was for "*the individual anywhere in the world judged to have made the greatest contribution to the advancement of the humanities*" and was worth $30,000. Britten gave a speech that pulled no punches about the role of a composer in modern society and the dangers of having great music available on tap through recordings. Further awards included the Gold Medal of the Royal Philharmonic Society and in 1965 Britten was appointed a member of the exclusive Order of Merit in the United Kingdom.

Britten visited the Soviet Union regularly over the next few years. The visit in October 1964, with the English Opera Group performing several of his operas, enabled him to spend more time with Shostakovich. The relationship with the great Russian composer, a notoriously shy man, blossomed. Back in Aldeburgh the 1967 Festival saw the opening of the Snape Maltings, converted to become a venue for the concerts and opera performances. Seating 800 people, it was opened by Queen Elizabeth II who afterwards had lunch with Britten at the Red House.

The Aldeburgh Festival was increasingly dominating Britten's life. Each year there were premieres of his recently composed works. Disaster struck at the beginning of the 1969 Festival when a fire started in the empty building and gutted the interior. Undeterred Britten switched the Festival to a local church and it was promised that the

Maltings would be rebuilt for the following year. Britten again participated actively in a second major fund-raising effort.

Britten bought Chapel House at Horham, some twenty miles from Aldeburgh so that he could have peace to compose. The new Maltings was ready for the 1970 Festival as promised, but with many improvements born of his experiences at the older venue. Britten's *Owen Wingrave*, a new opera commissioned by BBC Television was broadcast for the first time in May 1971. Within a week it had been seen throughout Europe and North America, demonstrating the potency of the television medium.

In 1971 Britten started serious work on the opera *Death in Venice*, based on Thomas Mann's book, and he completed it in April 1973. By then Britten was far from well. He had suffered from severe streptococcal infections of the throat in the past and this had caused a weakening of the heart, an illness similar to the one that killed Gustav Mahler. A heart operation was deemed necessary and took place in May 1973. The operation lasted six hours during which time Britten suffered a mild stroke which left him with a partially paralysed right hand. This gifted pianist never played again and could write only with the greatest of difficulty. After three weeks in hospital Britten returned to Chapel House to recuperate. He was too ill to attend the premiere of *Death in Venice* in mid-June.

Britten was now very frail and needed to husband his energy. The musical world celebrated his 60th birthday even if he was not able to. His sole objective was to compose while time remained to him. He now had a full time private nurse, Rita Thomson, who helped him enormously. His fifth canticle *The Death of St. Narcissus* was composed and he undertook several revisions of early works. Rostropovich, previously banned from foreign travel by the Soviet government because of his public support for the dissident Alexander Solzhenitsyn, was at last allowed to come to England for the long-delayed premiere of the *Cello Suite No. 3* in December 1974.

The 1975 Aldeburgh Festival premiered the *Suite on English Folk Tunes*, dedicated to the memory of Percy Grainger. The next Festival launched *Phaedra*, a cantata, and Britten was given a life peerage in June 1976, the first such tribute to an English composer. He completed his last work, *String Quartet No. 3*, in September. Britten grew increasingly

141

weak and passed away in the early hours of December 4, 1976, with Peter Pears and Rita Thomson by his side.

When Britten was buried in Aldeburgh cemetery three days later, the church service included two of his works. Three months later a service of thanksgiving for Britten was held in Westminster Abbey, with Peter Pears reading the lesson. In November 1978 a memorial was unveiled in the Abbey, next to that for Elgar and close to the grave of Henry Purcell.

Britten *The person*

Britten was lean, of medium height with short wavy hair and a prominent nose. He was intelligent, numerate and sporting. Keen on cricket he was also a good tennis player for many years. His homosexuality influenced the subject matter of many of his works, particularly the operas. He was always attracted to adolescent boys but had a genuine affinity with children.

He was the centre of attention from his earliest days, pushed forward by his mother's belief that he would be the fourth "B" after Bach, Beethoven and Brahms. He is said to have had an inferiority complex, which in view of his successful career is a remarkable thought. He was extremely gifted as a musician. As well as composing he was a pianist and conductor of the very highest quality. Orchestral musicians loved to play for him.

He was highly strung and extremely sensitive to criticism. There are many stories of his extreme reaction to perceived criticism and slights. He totally dropped W.H.Auden, an early intimate friend, because of the latter's criticism of the *Gloriana* text. Yet when he heard in 1973 that Auden had died Britten shed rare tears.

Naturally he preferred to have around him friends who were loyal, but those who transgressed were ruthlessly dropped. Those who remained were inspired by Britten and his music but the resulting Aldeburgh circle developed a reputation as a clique.

Britten preferred to be away from normal society. It is significant that he chose to live out in the depths of Suffolk for most of his life, close to the sea and to nature - and away from the intrigues of the musical establishment in London.

❧

Britten *His Music*

Here are my recommendations for a "Britten Starter Pack":

1 Four Sea Interludes from *Peter Grimes* contain some of the most evocative music of the sea ever written. *Dawn* makes its impact with high violins and brooding brass, the mood cold and calm – too calm! *Sunday morning* depicts the fishing village waking up, perky, pizzicato, the bustle starting. *Moonlight* is ravishing, quiet chords evoking a balmy night. *Storm* is appropriately violent, timpani having a field day, violins crying, trombones and bass drum terrifying, cymbals evoking dashing spray, before dying away as if spent – before a final eruption and a terrifying thundering down the scale, shrieking horns and trumpets prominent.

2 Serenade for tenor, horn & strings is a glorious example of a work of musical genius inspired by a performing genius, the horn player Denis Brain. Between a *Prologue and Epilogue* for solo horn lie six highly varied settings of works by poets including Tennyson, Blake and Yeats, the common theme being that of eventide. The horn is given a part equal to the tenor, either in duet or as accompanist. The writing for horn is taxing in the extreme, the results magnificent in the right hands. *Nocturne*, by Tennyson is perhaps most memorable for its horn (bugle) calls and the ebbing repeated phrase "*Dying.*" *Elegy* by Blake is given a profound setting, horn and tenor equal, the horn part again exceptional. The horn lets rip in the *Lyke-Wake Dirge* at the mention of Purgatory. The final song, *Sonnet*, is a hushed leave-taking.

3 Variations and Fugue on a Theme of Purcell (or *The Young Person's Guide to the Orchestra* as it is often called) sets out Purcell's theme immediately. It then proceeds to provide variations for each instrument in the woodwind, strings, brass and percussion before a brilliant fugue brings all together, one by one. The climax is the return of Purcell's theme in full majesty. The variations are both beautiful and stimulating, showing off each instrument and soloist to the full. The character of each instrument is also portrayed in Britten's music; so we have dancing violins, ravishing cellos and grumbling double basses and shimmering harp. It is a brilliant and entertaining work and every young person's parent should use it as an ideal introduction to classical music.

Orchestral Music

Now your appetite has been whetted, you are ready for the other key orchestral works.

Variations on a Theme of Frank Bridge is rightfully one of Britten's most popular works. Written for string orchestra, it opens with *Introduction and theme*, after which there are ten masterly and very different variations starting with a gorgeous *adagio*. You will, I am sure, have heard the scintillating *Aria Italiana*, note the extreme contrast with the *Funeral March* where Mahler's influence can be heard. *Chant* is intimate and eerie and highly original. The work concludes with *Fugue and finale*.

Symphony for Cello and Orchestra is perhaps Britten's most profound orchestral work, serious and dark. The opening *allegro maestoso* is pungent and dramatic, lyrical and modern at the same time. The orchestra is used with great delicacy. The *presto inquieto* opens with playful cello set against bizarre orchestral sounds. The heart of the work is the *adagio* which opens with rolling timpani, the cello making powerful statements against it before entering a magical world of muted strings and background woodwind. The timpani returns, followed by the full orchestra, tension rising towards the conclusion.

The formidable *Sinfonia da requiem* is in three movements, *Lacrymosa*, *Dies Irae* and *Requiem Aeternam*. The *Lacrymosa* opens with power and percussion and a funeral march of great intensity unfolds to a terrifying climax. The *Dies Irae* is a dance of death to brilliant brass and active percussion until there is a total disintegration. Flutes introduce the consoling theme of the finale, the landscape solitary. Violins enter to lead the music to a radiant climax for full orchestra that ebbs away.

The *Simple Symphony* is based on music Britten wrote between the ages of nine and twelve. It has four movements, *Boisterous Bourrée, Playful*

Pizzicato, *Sentimental Saraband*, and *Frolicsome Finale*. The titles say it all! The work is highly appealing, the *Saraband* particularly lovely.

In *Soirées Musicales* Britten arranges Rossini melodies into a five-movement dance suite. They are enormous fun, rip-roaring melodies, that make you ask *"Why don't we have tunes like these today?"* Later he produced a second suite *Matinées Musicales*. This too is a delight, particularly the opening *March* and the ensuing *Nocturne*.

Vocal & Choral Music

Britten's output in these categories was phenomenal and there are many masterpieces worthy of your attention, of which these are the principal ones!

Les Illuminations, settings of some exotic poems by Rimbaud, is a beautiful and highly appealing song cycle for high voice and string orchestra. The work opens with a delightful fanfare and the words *"J'ai seul la clef de cette parade sauvage."* (*I alone have the key to this uncivilised parade.*) The strings are vibrant, Britten's themes highly melodic, and the French language settings are seductive. Already in the *Interlude* one hears the origins of the *Peter Grimes Sea Interludes*. *Départ* makes a moving conclusion.

The choral *Spring Symphony* is one of Britten's most popular and typical works. In its four parts he uses carefully chosen but disparate texts from the 13th to 20th centuries. We start off in the glacial grip of winter, before trumpets announce *The merry cuckoo* and *Spring, the sweet Spring* with delightful bird imitations. In *Part Two* we move from *Welcome Maids of Honour* to a chilly remembrance of far-off events in Poland just before World War II. *Part Three* is light-hearted with a beautiful duet *Fair and fair*, followed by the exultant *Sound the flute*. *Part Four* is a festive waltz and a particular delight is the boys' chorus descant entry with the 13th century folk song *Sumer is icumen in*.

Britten's *War Requiem* is arguably one of the greatest musical masterpieces of the second half of the 20th Century. Its dual structures – Latin Requiem Mass interspersed with the profound poetry of Wilfred Owen, full orchestra and chamber orchestra/string quartet – create a unique work that is profoundly moving and speaks passionately about the diabolic folly of war.

The opening *Requiem aeternam*, classical and spare, is broken into by a tenor solo with the words "*What passing bells for these who die as cattle.*" Britten creates vivid pictures of war, percussion for the guns, trumpets as bugles. At the conclusion is a *Kyrie*, whilst a bell tolls. Next comes a central pillar of the work, the *Dies Irae*, opening with brass fanfares. The terrifying Latin text unfolds, Britten's music is restrained compared with the settings of Berlioz and Verdi. Into this breaks a sombre solo, "*Bugles sing, saddening the evening air.*" Later tenor and baritone sing the explosive "*Out there, we've walked quite friendly up to death.*" Later again the voices take separate passages culminating in the devastating "*Great gun towering t'ward heaven, about to curse.*"

After the *Offertorium*, *Sanctus* and *Agnus Dei* the work concludes with a gut-wrenching *Libera me*. After the return of the *Dies illa, dies irae* comes the meeting of tenor and baritone, (English Pears and German Fischer-Dieskau in the premiere), and "*I am the enemy you killed, my friend.*" to the accompaniment of a string quartet. Their final words, "*Let us sleep now.*" are overtaken by a vision of paradise and the final *Requiescat in pace*, "*May they rest in peace.*"

Hymn to St. Cecilia is for unaccompanied choir, Britten graphically colouring W. H. Auden's text. The style is ecclesiastical in the first of three sections, takes on a fairy-like lightness of touch in the middle section, and is orchestral in the fugal concluding section. *Oh dear white children casual as birds* – sung by a treble – is extraordinarily beautiful. The short chorus *Blessed Cecilia*, that concludes each section, departs finally in its most poignant guise.

A Boy was born is a set of variations on a theme, for mixed voices and boys' choir. The six texts chosen are mainly 15th and 16th century carols and Britten creates a powerful story-line, each variation unique in text, voices and mood. The third variation *Jesu, as Thou art our Saviour* has a particular peace and sonority, the fifth *In the bleak mid-winter* is as cold and brittle as you could ask. *Noël* closes the work in joy.

A Ceremony of Carols, for treble voices and harp, places nine carols between a *Procession* and a *Recession* reflecting the entry and departure of the choir. The carols are all of very early origin, Britten's settings a delight. The third *There is no Rose* is followed by two carols for treble solo, *That Yongë Child* hauntingly accompanied by harp, *Balulalow* a rocking lullaby. After an (at times) virtuosic interlude for solo harp, the

Ceremony concludes with three contrasting carols – *In freezing Winter Night*, where you almost shiver, to the joyful lilting *Spring carol*, and the rollicking *Deo Gracias*.

Our Hunting Fathers is a powerful "*Symphonic cycle for high voice and orchestra, with texts devised by W. H. Auden*", a devastating parable on the situation in Europe in 1936. Three poems *Rats Away!*, *Messalina* and *Dance of Death (Hawking for the Partridge)* are set between a *Prologue* and *Epilogue* written by Auden. The three concern the different relationships of man with animals – vermin, pet and prey. The orchestration is stunning, the *Dance of Death* horrifying, ending with the prescient words, "*German*", "*Jew*".

There are nine settings for tenor and piano in the exceptional *The Holy Sonnets of John Donne*, all profound religious meditations on death and repentance. Britten does justice to the sonnets with music that matches in inspiration and adds a further dimension of impact, whether it be the brilliant rushing moto perpetuos of the second and fourth or the beauty of the sixth, *Since she whom I loved*. *Death be not proud* concludes the cycle in magnificent defiance.

Nocturne is a setting of eight songs whose binding theme is sleep, (often nightmares). The poets range from Shakespeare to Wilfred Owen. Britten again shows he is a magician with song-cycles, and this one is essential listening, where the composer creates glorious pictures in sound. There is a strong chamber-music effect and Britten chooses one solo instrument for prominence in each song, whether it be bassoon, harp or timpani alongside the tenor. The mood is mainly reflective and somnolent.

In *Curlew River (A parable for Church Performance based on a Japanese Noh play)* Britten assumes "*an all male cast of ecclesiastics, a simple and austere staging in a church – a very limited instrumental accompaniment – and a moral story.*" In this case the story is of a demented mother seeking her lost child. The work takes its title from the River that the madwoman wants to cross, the other main characters are the Abbot and the Ferryman. It opens with the monks entering in procession to a Latin Hymn. The unfolding story is as important as the music – the libretto is largely sung speech and the musicians are often used to create the background. The madwoman finds the grave of her son, whose spirit speaks to her and releases her from her madness. The tension at times is palpa-

147

ble, there are marvellous effects throughout and the impact of the treble Spirit voice is considerable. A master of this highly original and very powerful form, Britten wrote two other parables, *The Burning Fiery Furnace* and *The Prodigal Son*.

Phaedra, a short cantata, was Britten's last work and concerns Phaedra's last hour as she poisons herself, having lusted after Hippolytus, the son of her husband, Theseus. It is a powerful work, charged with passion yet intimate and tragic.

Rejoice in the Lamb sets part of the poem *Jubilate Agno*, written by the 18th century poet Christopher Smart whilst he was confined in an asylum suffering from religious mania. In ten short sections and with organ accompaniment, this highly original, naïve and brilliant text receives a matching response from Britten. The concluding *For H* has a spirit extolling on the different musical instruments, an ideal text for Britten, before a quiet and serene conclusion of remarkable beauty. The work ends with a peaceful *Hallelujah*.

Britten wrote five works called *Canticles* (described as extended settings of a single poem on a spiritual subject) over a period of nearly 30 years. *Canticle 1, My beloved is mine*, for tenor and piano, has 17th century text. *Canticle II*, my favourite, is from a 15th century Miracle Play, *Abraham and Isaac*. For alto and tenor, it has quite gorgeous harmonies for the two voices. *Canticle III, Still falls the Rain*, is from Edith Sitwell's *The raids, 1940 Nighted Dawn*. Very powerful, it is set for tenor, horn and piano and is a profound reflection on the unchanging evil in the world. The tenor and horn finally come together in the last stanza, the piano silent until the final bars. *Canticle IV, Journey of the Magi* by T. S. Eliot, appropriately has three voices, tenor, counter-tenor and baritone, and *Canticle V, The Death of St. Narcissus*, also by T. S. Eliot, continues the variety of performers, this time for tenor and harp. It is an intense and concise work.

Operas

Britten became famous with the launch of *Peter Grimes* and it has remained the only one of his operas to stake a firm place in the international repertoire. The others include more than one masterpiece but their subject matter is often quirky, related to themes attractive to

Britten. The libretti are always dramatic and serious but there is not a romantic soprano in sight.

Peter Grimes is set in the Borough on the east coast of England and opens with the inquest into the death of a young boy apprenticed to Peter Grimes, a local fisherman. Grimes is cleared but the townsfolk are suspicious. A replacement boy is needed and Ellen Orford, the schoolmistress, brings home John, whom Grimes immediately takes to his sea-shore hut in a raging storm. A few weeks later Ellen meets John and discovers he is bruised and has torn clothes. Later the townsfolk go to Grime's hut to investigate – Grimes rushes away to avoid them, taking John with him, but the lad slips and is dashed to death on the rocks. The townsfolk find nothing. A few days later John's jersey is washed up on the beach and the Mayor orders the arrest of Grimes. Ellen Orford and a friend, Captain Bulstrode, go to find Grimes, newly returned from sea and in an appalling state, nearly out of his mind. Bulstrode proposes to Grimes that he takes his boat out to sea and scuttles it, remaining on board, and this he does. In the Borough a boat is reported as sinking way out at sea but is ignored. Life is back to normal.

Britten creates music that maintains a marvellously evocative and often claustrophobic atmosphere – this is East Anglian angst to match the East European angst of Janáček's *Katya Kabanová*! After the inquest the *First Sea Interlude* opens *Act 1*, violins and trombones introducing the chorus. The magnificent *Sea Interludes* play a key role in setting the scene and atmosphere throughout the opera. Arias as such are few. Ellen's first solo makes its impact through the orchestral accompaniment, often powerful, and this remains Britten's style throughout as he paints mood and tone pictures with great skill. In Bulstrode's *"Look the storm comes"* the chorus adds a further dramatic dimension, and crowd scenes throughout are as important as the key characters. Village life is heard in songs from the pub, a village dance and a hymn from the church. The opera ends with a noble chorus about the sea.

Billy Budd is about three people, Billy, the newly press-ganged handsome and idealistic sailor, Claggart, the bully of a bosun, and Captain Vere of the warship Indomitable. The year is 1797. Claggart resents Billy's goodness and good looks and determines to destroy him by accusing him in front of Captain Vere of trying to create a mutiny. Billy, shocked, strikes Claggart and kills him. Billy is court-martialled, and the moral dilemma of his punishment takes over. Vere in the end refuses to save him and Billy is hanged from the yard-arm.

Billy Budd inevitably has an all-male cast and the music is much more melodic than in Peter Grimes. The mood on the ship is lively, the music imaginative, particularly the brass. Billy's "*King of the world*" has a full orchestra and makes a great introduction. Vere, too, has a formidable entrance with brass and chorus. In the opening to *Scene 2* in *Act 2* Britten creates a powerful prelude and evocative chorus before a surging sea shanty. Claggart's "*O beauty*" reeks of evil, accentuated by his bass voice. *Act 3* opens with the excitement of preparing for battle against a French ship but the real drama starts in *Scene 2* when the orchestra creates a formidable picture of Vere's meeting with Claggart and Budd. The tension of the court-martial is palpable and as Vere goes to tell Billy the verdict the orchestra is given an extraordinary passage of 34 chords. The conclusion is riveting, Billy's moving final aria and the execution, and the revulsion of the crew – a silent chorus – is expressed by an orchestral crescendo and diminuendo.

The *Rape of Lucretia* takes place in Rome in the 6th century B.C. Tarquinius, son of the king, becomes obsessed with Lucretia, the faithful wife of Collatinus. He visits her and rapes her and when Collinatus arrives the next morning Lucretia stabs herself, in spite of her husband's understanding. Apart from the central characters there is a major role for male and female choruses, commentating, drawing lessons and even influencing. To this powerful heterosexual tale Britten brings most apt music with a small chamber orchestra. Listen to the tranquil but alert music for female chorus as Lucretia lies sleeping, the cor anglais and exquisite cellos as Lucretia comes to meet her husband for the last time, and their emotionally laden final conversation.

Death in Venice is based on Thomas Mann's short tale of a man, Aschenbach, and his obsession with a beautiful young boy, Tadzio, whom he sees in Venice. They do not meet but the outcome is Aschenbach's corruption and death. For this intense but simple story which was obviously a situation with which he could identify, Britten creates a delicate but brilliant musical palette.

If you like these Britten operas the others well worth exploring are *Albert Herring*, *Gloriana*, *The Turn of the Screw*, and *A Midsummer Night's*

*Dream.*The early *Paul Bunyan* is completely different, written in a folksy, American style.

Concertos

In our competitive and judgmental age Britten's concertos have not been deemed attractive enough to gain the places in the repertoire that those of his rough contemporaries Shostakovich and Prokofiev have achieved.

The riveting and much undervalued *Violin Concerto* opens intensely, a Spanish rhythm and motto prevalent throughout the profound ensuing lament – listen to the passage when the violin enunciates the rhythm whilst muted strings intone the first theme. *The scherzo* is a brilliant and macabre dance, the concluding *passacaglia* opening with solo violin, trombones having the theme. The variations are like a tragic story, one episode giving way to another, the orchestration superb, the effect heartbreaking.

The *Piano Concerto* is, in Britten's words, "*a bravura concerto with orchestral accompaniment.*" It is a shame that Britten did not return to this genre in his maturity. In four movements, the opening *Toccata* rushes constantly forward, always brilliant. The *Waltz* has a spectral element to it, hushed in part, almost – but not quite – playful, but Mahlerian grotesque at times. The *Impromptu* opens in total devastation, the piano eventually awaking to accompany a riveting passacaglia. The *March* grows from nothing into a banal brass band performance, with some profounder passages, both perhaps appropriate to the year 1938.

Chamber Music

Britten's principal chamber music was written for the string quartet or for solo cello. His *Cello Suites* were inspired by the performing genius of Mstislav Rostropovich and perhaps the composing genius of his friend Shostakovich.These three works are in a hereditary line from Bach. *Suite No.1* has six movements unified by a *Canto (Sostenuto e largamente)* which opens, comments on, and closes the work. The *Lamento* exudes solitude and not a little desolation. Britten always brings variety; he moves through a pizzicato movement, a march, a drone to a final *moto perpetuo.*

Suite No. 2 is more intense and is a formidable work. It opens with a solitary and dramatic *largo* followed by a *fugue* that seems to create itself, a scurrying *scherzo*, an eerie *andante* and a *cinchona (chaconne)* with twelve variations.

Suite No.3 is considered to be the most personal of the suites. It has nine movements, all short bar the concluding one which is nearly as long as all the others together. Britten uses Russian themes to create a masterpiece celebrating friendship and integrity.

Britten's three *String Quartets* are all accessible works. *String Quartet No.1* opens with ethereal strings and a pizzicato cello before an energetic *allegro vivo*, providing repeated and attractive contrast. A ghostly *allegretto* is followed by an extended *andante calmo* of great beauty and intensity. A brief and whizzing finale has some highly original effects.

String Quartet No.2 is a tribute to Henry Purcell. It has two substantial movements, an *allegro* and a giant *chacony* on either side of a short *vivace*. The first movement is serious and discursive, the second rushing and brilliant, and the concluding *chacony* is a most profound utterance.

String Quartet No.3 has five movements, ending with a *passacaglia* entitled *La Sereñissima*, since Britten had completed the work whilst holidaying in Venice. The opening *Duets* has some gorgeous echo effects, *Solo*, the third movement commences with an initial plaintive accompanied violin before the mood goes quite mad. After a *burlesque* we arrive at the climax, the *passacaglia*, which is profound, introspective music.

10

SHOSTAKOVICH

Shostakovich *His Life*

Dmitri Dmitriyevich Shostakovich was born on September 12, 1906, in St. Petersburg, the son of Dmitri and Sofiya Shostakovich. His father was an engineer who worked at the Palace of Weights and Measures, founded by the famous chemist Mendeleyev and his mother was the daughter of a goldmine manager in Eastern Siberia. The parents already had a daughter, Mariya, and another, Zoya, was to follow in 1908. During this troubled time in Russia, with widespread unrest and poverty under Tsar Nicolas, the Shostakovich family was amongst the better off, with the use of a country house and that recent invention, an automobile.

Sofiya was an excellent pianist, having studied at the St. Petersburg Conservatoire and she ensured that her children had a musical upbringing. Their father had a good singing voice. The young Dmitri's first major musical experiences were visits to the opera to hear *Eugen Onegin* and *Tsar Saltan*. As soon as her children reached the age of nine Sofiya started to give them piano lessons and within two days of starting with the somewhat sickly Dmitri, she knew she had an "*outstandingly gifted boy*". All three children would eventually go to the Conservatoire. Soon Dmitri began his first efforts at composition and in 1915 he started at a private school where he proved to be a hard-working student.

The civil unrest that was growing in Russia came to a head in the Revolution of 1917. Demonstrations broke out at the beginning of the year in St. Petersburg and Shostakovich never forgot the sight of a Cossack hacking down a young boy with his sabre during one of the street riots. In March Shostakovich composed a funeral march in memory of the victims of the Revolution but it was October before Lenin emerged as the leader of the new Soviet Union. The next few years were to see continued strife and hardship, particularly for well-off people like the Shostakovich family who had many of their possessions

confiscated. They now lived in an apartment in the city and Sofiya sheltered many people in difficulties.

During all this turbulence Shostakovich was developing as a talented pianist and was just 13 when he started attending the Conservatoire in addition to his academic studies. Glazunov was in charge and soon recognising Shostakovich's potential as a composer, he took a strong interest in the youngster's progress. Shostakovich's musical education therefore combined composition with training to be a concert pianist. At home Sofiya regularly organised parties where 30 people would dance until the early hours of the morning, for which her son would often play the piano.

When his father died in 1922 the family fortunes declined further but Sofiya Shostakovich was a strong woman, determined to do the best for her children. Her sister and brother-in-law moved into the family apartment and Sofiya took a job as a shop cashier. Mariya had to work and Shostakovich had to take a job as a pianist in a local cinema to help the family survive. His health was not good as he suffered from malnutrition, anaemia and overwork.

Shostakovich became a full-time student at the Conservatoire in 1922 and was a model student with a particular affinity for the music of Beethoven. By the time he graduated in 1924 he had become an exceptional pianist and a highly talented composer. He was blessed with a phenomenal memory and was able to compose a full score in his head. Life at the Conservatoire was not easy for the place was full of political intrigue, and in addition Shostakovich's talent and background provoked extreme hostility from. some of his fellow students. Brushing this off Shostakovich started work on a symphony in 1924 and completed it whilst undertaking a post-graduate course.

His teachers were sufficiently impressed to arrange for a performance of the symphony by the Leningrad Philharmonic (the city had changed its name from St Petersburg) under Nikolai Malko. The work was premiered in May 1926 and made an enormous impact. Shostakovich was given a long and loud ovation – a great composer had arrived! The symphony was performed in Moscow shortly afterwards, in Berlin the following year and in America in 1928.

After Shostakovich had completed his studies the next major development was his appointment as music adviser and pianist at the theatre of the controversial director Vsevolod Meyerhold. There Shostakovich became something of a musical revolutionary, writing music for the theatre and films that shocked many people. With his newfound fame he was also soon giving interviews, declaring himself amongst the revolutionaries. He had his first brush with the authorities after composing an orchestral arrangement of the foxtrot *"Tea for Two"*. Composed in less than 45 minutes as a bet with Malko, this popular piece aligned too much with the decadent West and Shostakovich had to write the first of what were to be many apologies to the bureaucrats.

Symphony No.2, dedicated to the revolution, was premiered in 1927 and a first opera, *The Nose*, based on Gogol's satire in which an arrogant bureaucrat's nose achieves its own identity, was completed in 1930. In 1932 Shostakovich married Nina Vasilyevna Varzar whom he had met some years before. His first love had been Tatyana Glivenko whom he had met in 1923, but she had tired of waiting for Shostakovich to commit himself and married someone else. She nearly left her husband for Shostakovich but again he vacillated and when she became pregnant he married Nina. They had a difficult relationship and divorced within a few years, only to re-marry. They were to have two children, Galya, born in 1936, and Maxim, born two years later. Theirs was an open marriage. For much of the time there was another man in Nina's life and Shostakovich had at least one serious affair.

In the early thirties Shostakovich was principally a man of the theatre and the opera *Lady Macbeth of Mtsensk* was his next major work. Premiered in Leningrad in 1934 it proved a great success and was also performed in New York and London. Unfortunately Stalin, dictator of the Soviet Union since Lenin's death in 1924, went to see it in January 1936 and two days later the national newspaper Pravda carried a long piece denouncing the opera under the title *"Muddle instead of music, Chaos instead of order"*. Rumour said it was written by Stalin but it was more likely the work of a high-ranking bureaucrat.

Shostakovich now experienced the full force of a totalitarian regime. His works were no longer performed and many musicians and so-called friends felt obliged to ostracise him. There were numerous debates in which his reputation was besmirched. It was an appalling time for him and his family but there were true friends who supported him. To one he said *"Even if they chop my hands off I will still continue to compose music – albeit I have to hold the pen with my teeth."* Realistically Shostakovich decided to withdraw his recently completed *Fourth Symphony*, a formidable and difficult work that was to remain locked away until 1961.

In 1937 Shostakovich was ordered to attend a meeting with the NKVD, later known as the KGB. He was interrogated about a friend, the music-loving Marshal Tukhachevsky, whom Stalin was to execute. Enormous pressure was put on Shostakovich to implicate the Marshal in a plot to assassinate Stalin. When he refused he was given the weekend to reconsider his statement. He spent the time putting his affairs in order, expecting the worst, but when he returned on the Monday his interviewer had himself been arrested. Shostakovich heard nothing more of the matter!

Shostakovich's redemption in the eyes of Stalin came through the composer's *Fifth Symphony* which was given the by-line *"A Soviet artist's reply to just criticism"* by a journalist. It was premiered by the Leningrad Philharmonic under Mravinsky, who was to become the leading interpreter of Shostakovich's orchestral music. This more accessible music, with its superficially affirmative conclusion, allowed Shostakovich back into favour. He was increasingly drawn to chamber music and he commenced the first of his magnificent series of string quartets in 1938. The *Sixth Symphony* followed in 1940 as well as the *Piano Quintet* which won a Stalin prize worth 100,000 roubles, a very substantial sum.

War erupted in June 1941 as Hitler's German army invaded its ally the Soviet Union. Shostakovich volunteered for the army but was turned down. Instead he became a fireman protecting the Conservatoire, which allowed him to continue composing. Leningrad was soon under siege from the advancing Germans and Shostakovich was evacuated from the city at the beginning of October.

Shostakovich spent the next period of the war in the safety of Kuibyshev, well to the east of Moscow. Here many Soviet artists, including the Bolshoi Ballet, were housed in difficult circumstances. Shostakovich completed his *Seventh Symphony* and dedicated it to the city of Leningrad. This graphic and inspirational work was premiered in March 1942 by the Bolshoi Orchestra and, amazingly, was performed in the besieged city of Leningrad five months later. The score was smuggled to the West and quickly achieved fame in the free world.

Shostakovich moved to Moscow as the Germans were thrown back, and he took up the position of Professor of Composition at the

Conservatoire. He started work on another mighty work, the *Eighth Symphony*. The family now had access to the Composer's House of the Union of Soviet Composers, a haven where he could work and mix with other musicians. Shostakovich would retire to a hut in the forest to compose and there were great expectations of his *Ninth Symphony*, coinciding with the end of the war. Shostakovich hinted at a great *Victory Symphony* with chorus and soloists, which was what Stalin wanted, but instead he produced a short, relatively light, purely orchestral work. This deliberate gesture of defiance invoked Stalin's wrath yet again.

After the war the state began to exert more pressure on artists, particularly poets and composers. Zhdanov, who had led the Leningrad resistance, organised a witch hunt directed particularly against Prokofiev and Shostakovich, Russia's greatest composers. A conference of composers was held in 1948 where Shostakovich was obliged to toe the party line, ending with an apology and the following words, whose interpretation can be grovelling or dripping with sarcasm, as one chooses. "*I think that our three days' discussion will be of the greatest value, especially if we closely study Comrade Zhdanov's speech. I, no doubt like others, should like to have the text of his speech. A close study of this remarkable document should help us greatly in our work.*"

Shostakovich's situation was now worse than it had been in 1936, with his works effectively banned from performance. He was dismissed from the Leningrad Conservatoire and was close to suicide for a while as his income vanished. The famous cellist Rostropovich has recounted how Prokofiev approached him, "*Slava, I have no money left to buy our breakfast. We have nothing to eat.*" Shostakovich returned to composition with his *Twenty-Four Preludes and Fugues for Piano* but the *Violin Concerto*, written for David Oistrakh, remained in a drawer.

However Stalin needed Shostakovich as an example of Soviet culture against the West. One day early in 1949 the composer received a phone call from Stalin who wanted the composer to travel to the USA for the Congress of Peace and Culture. Shostakovich pointed out that it would be difficult for him as his symphonies were played in America but were forbidden in his homeland. "*How do you mean forbidden? Forbidden by whom?*" demanded Stalin and in a few days the ban was lifted and the State Commission for Repertoire was reprimanded. Shostakovich was given instruction by a so-called sociologist from the Conservatoire on how to toe the party line!

Shostakovich was forced to be a Soviet delegate on various cultural missions between 1949 and 1952. In the USA he had to denounce Western music, much to his embarrassment. He continued to compose but withheld most of his works from performance, waiting for better times. Stalin died unexpectedly in 1953 and Shostakovich celebrated the tyrant's death with the magnificent *Tenth Symphony*, arguably his greatest. Little by little oppression and censorship were lifted.

By 1954 Shostakovich had a large apartment in Moscow, rented a state dacha 30 miles outside the city, owned a car and earned enough money to live a comfortable life. But his wife Nina died in that same year and his mother soon after. The *Seventh String Quartet* was dedicated to Nina's memory. Friends and family were much concerned as to how Shostakovich would cope alone. Within two years he had married Margarita Kainova but the marriage quickly failed.

Kruschev's denunciation of Stalin was an important liberating event and a number of exceptional performers, particularly the pianists Sviatoslav Richter and Emil Gilels, the violinist David Oistrakh and the cellist Mstislav Rostropovich, emerged to stimulate Shostakovich. Oistrakh premiered the *Violin Concerto No. 1* in 1955, seven years after its completion.

Shostakovich was encouraged to write two symphonies celebrating the revolutions of 1905 (*No. 11*, premiered in 1957) and 1917 (*No. 12*, premiered in 1961). At first he planned to make the latter a satire on Lenin but he got cold feet at the last minute and modified it. For Rostropovich he wrote the exceptional *Cello Concerto No. 1*, premiered in 1959. In 1960 and much to the disappointment of many of his friends, Shostakovich was persuaded to join the Communist Party, which was a success for Kruschev. The *Fourth Symphony* finally came out of Shostakovich's drawer in 1961, its message from the 1930s making a profound impact.

In 1962 Shostakovich was living in a five-room apartment in premises for musicians with his married children, and next to the Rostropovich family. He met Irena Supinskaya, a 27-year-old literary editor, whose father had been killed in one of Stalin's purges. She was already married but quickly divorced her elderly husband to marry

Shostakovich. From then on she organised his life and cared for him. In the *Thirteenth Symphony* the composer set poems by Yevgeni Yevtushenko, but the content of the poems was too much for the State and for Mravinsky who didn't dare to conduct it. The audience's response at the premiere was ecstatic but the work was immediately blacklisted.

Lady Macbeth of Mtsensk was discreetly resurrected as *Katerina Ismailova* in Moscow. The tickets advertised Rossini's *The Barber of Seville* as even under its new name *Lady Macbeth* was still banned; however it was substituted for the Rossini opera just before the curtain went up! Again Shostakovich's music had an exceptional reception and there were no objections when the opera was performed under its own name two weeks later.

Igor Stravinsky was invited to the Soviet Union in 1962. His main ambition was to meet a reluctant Shostakovich. They met twice but had little in common and conversation was stilted. In contrast Shostakovich developed a close friendship with Benjamin Britten whom he had first met in 1959. They had an immediate rapport and their relationship lasted for the rest of Shostakovich's life, with Shostakovich visiting Britten's Aldeburgh Festival in 1962.

In 1965 Shostakovich was diagnosed as having a form of poliomyelitis that affected his nerve-endings and bones. He also had a heart condition and the gradual loss of the strength of his right hand forced him to give up the piano. After a heart attack in 1966, when he spent two months in hospital, he aged suddenly and his health never recovered. His sixtieth birthday was celebrated with the premiere of the *Cello Concerto No.2* played by Rostropovich and the composer received numerous honours including the Order of Lenin. For the rest of his life he was to receive many more honours from around the world.

Shostakovich composed his *Violin Concert No.2* as a 60th birthday present for David Oistrakh and much of his creative energy went into his series of string quartets. In 1969 he completed the *Fourteenth Symphony*. Dedicated to Britten, it was premiered and recorded at a closed concert in Moscow in June. During the performance one of Shostakovich's former persecutors died of a heart attack!

The persecution of dissidents increased in the Soviet Union after the invasion of Czechoslovakia in 1968 but Shostakovich, unlike

Rostropovich, did little to support them. He was not proud to add his name to a letter condemning Solzhenitsyn and Sakharov, but he did so, creating resentment amongst many.

The Nose was revived in 1971 in a student performance and again three years later under the conductor Rozhdestvensky. Shostakovich was very ill but attended the rehearsals and the first performance, which was for him a moving experience. He continued to work in spite of declining health and his last work was the *Viola Sonata*. Shostakovich was now suffering from lung cancer amongst other ailments and he was taken into hospital in early July 1975. He returned home a month later only to have to return into care a few days later. He died unexpectedly at 7.30 p.m. on Saturday August 9, the main cause of his death being cancer.

The funeral was a grand Soviet affair held on August 14. Shostakovich's open coffin lay in the Grand Hall of the Moscow Conservatoire in the morning with recorded music playing in the background – all Moscow's orchestras were on holiday. At 1 p.m. speeches were made, most affirming the status of Shostakovich as a communist. Afterwards the entourage left for the Novodevechi Cemetery where more speeches were given before the coffin was nailed down and Shostakovich was at last at peace.

Shostakovich *The person*

Shostakovich was thin and quite tall. He had copper-coloured hair and grey eyes almost hidden behind the extremely thick glasses necessary for his myopia. For much of his life he looked much younger than his years.

He had a highly sensitive and nervous disposition, his hands were always agitated and he was a chain-smoker. He was tense in all but the most relaxed circumstances with intimate friends. He would chew his nails and fingers, stare at people but then abruptly avert his gaze if noticed. Often his mind would appear to be elsewhere, as he was probably composing in his head.

He was a keen soccer fan and liked his vodka, though he did not have a strong head for it. He was extremely fond of literature and knew large passages of some of Russia's great writers by heart.

A very private person and shy, he rarely betrayed his feelings and thoughts. He would present an external diffidence that contrasted with firmly held personal views. He would never impose those views in conversation but would usually get his own way on personal and musical matters. He would apparently accept criticism of his music openly but seldom changed a score.

Shostakovich was a very honest person, modest, with a high degree of integrity. He was a realist who saw the truth of the world he had the misfortune to live in. Pessimism seemed the most appropriate perspective.

He was very supportive of friends and colleagues and often put himself at risk to help them. He didn't expect anything in return, recognising that people had to make severe compromises to survive in Stalin's Soviet Union. Thus he considered that the public statements he was required to make by the State, for example denouncing Western music, as totally meaningless. Some thought him cowardly and certainly he was much more compliant in his later years, which was a little surprising as Stalin was dead. He developed a strong sense of irony so that opposite meanings could be read into some utterances, leaving the listener to make his own choice.

In his music lies, for those with perception, the most damning indictment of Stalin's regime. This was Shostakovich's ultimate courageous triumph over the tyrant he hated.

Shostakovich *His Music*

Shostakovich chose to write music in the traditional forms of classical music, yet never looked backwards in his style. Remarkably, he combined his progressiveness with a deep emotional content easily recognisable to lovers of the great 19th century composers. For him Beethoven was the dominant influence, but he was also very much influenced by Mahler. Few other composers can compete with his claim to be the greatest classical composer of the 20th century

For an introduction to his music here is my recommended "Shostakovich Starter Pack":

1 Symphony No.5 The opening with its motto theme is immediately dramatic and despairing. The gripping movement unfolds like a sad story, the orchestration spare for much of the time. A crude march takes over and climaxes brutally although some solace is provided by flute and horn before the bleak ending. The brief *scherzo* is burlesque in nature, highly rhythmic and shrill but for a wry *trio* led by a solo violin. The intense and moving *largo* has long thematic passages, the mood being one of sadness, tumbling to despair in the climax. The *finale* opens with a fast march, timpani thundering, before setting off at an even faster pace, eventually to arrive at a major key peroration that represents a hollow victory.

2 Cello Concerto No.1 is an immensely appealing work, its quirky rhythmic four-note motto immediately launched by the soloist and dominating the opening *allegretto*. Once heard, never forgotten! The substantial *moderato* is gently lyrical for the main part, the cello rhapsodic, the orchestra hushed, the melodies as beautiful as any produced by Shostakovich. After a brief climax the music seems to vanish into space, succeeded by a long and difficult solo cadenza, ruminative at first then gathering pace to break into the condensed final movement. It rushes along, finally integrating the first theme of the work triumphantly into the ending.

3 Piano Concerto No.1 for Piano, String orchestra and Trumpet is an exuberant work in four movements. In the first, rich in melody, Shostakovich quotes from Beethoven and Haydn. The *lento* is an oasis of beauty, gently rocking and awaiting the piano entry. Next we are into Bach, before skipping forward brilliantly to the rip-roaring final movement. Great fun, most ingenious, and guaranteed to bring the house down!

The Symphonies

Shostakovich composed one of the great symphonic series; its unusually wide variety ranges from profound masterpieces to lighter ones and from pure orchestral to vocal and choral. Shostakovich used his symphonies as his main statements, they chart his development and experiences and make a vivid and powerful listening experience. After *No. 5* I recommend you go straight to *No. 10*, considered to be his greatest.

Symphony No. 10 opens with a long *moderato*, a movement of deep intimate introspection. The themes are extended, the colours dark, the sounds rising to screeching full orchestra before falling back pensively. Next comes a brutal *allegro* reputed to depict Stalin, fast-moving and intensely rhythmic. The following *allegretto* is light-touched and melancholic, with private moments giving way to a full orchestral climax before vanishing into silence. The finale, *andante – allegro*, opens eerily, oboe over hushed strings. Into this brooding mood gradually emerges a jaunty clarinet, whose theme is abducted by the full orchestra. With the massed power of the orchestra the theme brushes aside aggressive interventions until cellos enter with a consoling melody – rare for the composer. Forced jollity prevails – the macabre is not far away – just listen for the bassoon that leads the final peroration.

When you have experienced the greatest of Shostakovish's symphonies I now recommend that you follow his development. *Symphony No. 1* is the most popular of the early symphonies. It has delightful effects in its opening bars as if the composer has just entered a magical world and is flexing his muscles. The first movement is playful, as is the second, a *scherzo*. The *lento* gives a foretaste of some of the great slow movements to come, oboe leading the threnody. A snare drum announces the dramatic last movement, a brooding opening giving way to a rushing *allegro molto*, with volcanic eruptions and interludes for solo violin and cello. The thrilling conclusion builds from the latter and is dominated by brass fanfares.

Symphony No. 2 and *Symphony No. 3* are like symphonic poems, each with a choral ending and no break between sections. *No. 2* is titled *To October*, and *No. 3* is *The Fourth of May*. Both are "party political" but well worth hearing for Shostakovich's imaginative music and the rousing choruses at the conclusions

Symphony No. 4 carries the spirit of Mahler. It is enormously powerful with an extreme range of moods and effects. The long first movement opens with shrieks that give way to a pounding mechanical machine, contrasting with the later desolate bassoon. The unfolding saga is riveting. What is going to come next? The short scherzo-like second movement has an imaginative and eerie ending, dominated by light percussion, and the concluding movement is also of great originality. A slow opening section builds to a march-like climax, followed by a remorseless *scherzo* that gathers pace and volume before ebbing into a spectral but attractive *nachtmusik*. The music then goes back the way it came, through great climaxes to a hushed conclusion. Wow!

Symphony No. 6 has an unusual form, a long *largo* followed by two much shorter fast movements but don't let that put you off. The *largo* is serious and intense, brooding at times, searing at others. The second movement is light-hearted and brilliant, the last is related to Prokofiev's *Classical Symphony* in its apparent swirling delight, but there are deeper undertones of cynicism similar to the conclusion of the *Fifth* with the repeated chant for the horns.

Symphony No. 7, Leningrad is another mighty work, its partial composition and a performance under the German siege inevitably contributing to its impact. The 30 minute-long opening *allegretto* is notable for the arrival of the simple tune that grows Bolero-like into a horrifying march, the overall effect shattering. The long quiet close has a sense of eerie stillness. The *scherzo* is affirmative, the *adagio* has a Mahlerian beauty and sense of peace. It leads straight into the last movement, steadily transforming into a life and death struggle and a final grandiose major key peroration. Overwhelming in the circumstances!

Symphony No. 8 is one of the most powerful of Shostakovich's symphonies and was referred to by the composer, along with the *Seventh*, as his *Requiem*. In C minor, it has five movements. The opening of the very long first movement is pessimistic and spare, with bleak strings. The movement slowly gathers pace and volume, brass, drums and shrieking piccolos enter to create a horrifying and enormous sound of terror, with drum rolls and brass fanfares before bleakness returns. The *allegretto* is a scherzo and opens with an example of the diabolical machine-like march that Shostakovich does so well. The following movement is another scherzo, very closely related and even more machine-like and violent – terrifying as it rushes to the concluding climax and the beginning of the mysterious *largo*, where quiet instruments are heard over double basses. The concluding *allegretto* brings a pastoral mood and ostensible light relief until the terror returns briefly. As with many Shostakovich symphonic endings the levity is hollow.

Symphony No.9 is great fun, a wry, witty and concise work in five movements. The sprightly opening *allegro* is memorable for the regular appearance of an intrusive motif on the trombone. The second, *moderato*, is largely quiet and rhapsodic, like chamber-music. Woodwind are again prominent in the bustling little *presto* that follows, where the trumpet theme stands out. The movement runs straight into the powerful and sombre brass intonations of the *largo*, which in turn evaporates into the jolly but deliberately banal finale – a sign of the composer having fun.

Symphony No.11, like its successor, is a programmatic work, entitled *The Year 1905*, when the Tsar's troops fired on unarmed demonstrators in front of the Winter Palace in St.Petersburg. The opening *adagio: The Palace Square* is bleak in the extreme but moving, the second, *allegro: 9 January*, vividly depicts the approach of the demonstrators and their slaughter. Next comes a powerful requiem, *adagio: In memoriam*, a great elegy led by the violas, and the symphony concludes with an *allegro non troppo*, a brash semi-triumphant conclusion except for a haunting warning led by the oboe towards the end.

Symphony No.12 The Year 1917 was dedicated to Lenin. The four movements run into each other. The opening, *Revolutionary Petrograd*, is urgent, bustling, full of energy, lower strings dominating, until an uplifting theme is taken up by the violins and the full orchestra - it will appear throughout the work. *Razliv* depicts Lenin's hide-out and is a brooding slow movement. *Aurora*, the battleship that started the Revolution, grows out of timpani strokes into the battle itself, the theme triumphant as the music enters the celebratory uplands of the *Dawn of Humanity*, tension and terror vanquished but not forgotten. The theme is given an extended peroration.

Symphony No.13 Babi Yar is a deeply moving and very Russian work. Set for bass, male chorus and orchestra, its five movements have texts written by Yevgeny Yevtushenko, all viewed as subversive by the Soviet regime, but deadly accurate in their irony. *Babi Yar* is the title of the first movement, and the name of a ravine outside Kiev where the Nazis massacred more than 100,000 people, mainly Jews, in 1941. Yevtushenko's poem, strongly against anti-Semitism, is harrowing and

Shostakovich's music, violent or compassionate where appropriate, does it full justice,. The other movements are called *Humour, In the store, Fears,* and *Careers.* In this symphony Shostakovich at last shows his true feelings openly, partnering a poet of genius and greater social conscience and courage.

Symphony No.14 is a setting of 11 poems for soprano, bass, string orchestra and percussion, the common theme being death. Titles include *De Profundis, The Suicide, The Poet's Death.* A superb song cycle, the moods and meanings of the texts are well captured, the orchestration masterly.

Shostakovich's last symphony was written for a small orchestra. In it the composer quotes from Rossini in the first movement and Wagner in the last to produce an enigmatic but highly typical work in four movements. It is as if this great composer of symphonies said "This will keep them guessing". The *Fifteenth* is superbly entertaining and witty and particularly moving in the *adagio* second movement.

Concertos

Cello Concerto No.2 is far less extrovert than its predecessor, but no less masterly and even more original. It opens with a long *largo*, in a mood of gentle and private contemplation, with the musical ideas often treated in chamber-music style. Half-way through, the orchestra becomes playful for a period, the extended percussion section contributing before a serene ending. A brief *allegretto*, reminiscent of the opening of *No.1*, leads into the last movement, also *allegretto* but this time more substantial, launched by a highly original fanfare from the horns accompanied by a drum roll. There are passages of intimate beauty as well as playfulness before the fanfares return to lead a jolly dance for a short period. The conclusion is dream-like, the cello left to play alone with agitated percussion

Piano Concerto No.2 is a joyful work, its jaunty piano theme declaring its character. The *andante* is a throwback to the days of gorgeous slow movements, a rapt background onto which the piano drops pearls. The following *allegro* is sprightly, brilliant and rhythmic, and has an exhilarating conclusion.

The Assault on Beautiful Gorky is a one-movement mini-concerto from the film music for the *The Unforgettable Year 1919*, written in 1951.

167

It has the broad sweep of *Lara's theme* from the film *Dr. Zhivago* and is truly up-lifting – an exposure of a side of Shostakovich we rarely see. Maybe for him it was written-to-measure but there's none of the sarcastic commentary with which he signposts his *"writing for the politburo"* music.

Violin Concerto No. 1 opens on the same profound scale as the later *Symphony No. 10*. The first of the four movements is brooding and mysterious, with cellos and basses dominating the orchestra at first. The *scherzo* is bustling. Solo violin and wind instruments cut across the orchestra; it is hard work at first but soon we are flying to an exhilarating conclusion. Next comes a *passacaglia*, a form much favoured by the composer. It appears as a powerful statement on the brass initially, then turns inward to become a superb slow movement. The concerto ends with a *burlesque* – this is wild music leading to a stunning conclusion!

Violin Concerto No. 2 is a much more sombre affair, written towards the end of the composer's life. The opening *moderato* is dark and fierce, though with its delicate moments with solo horn. The mood of the *adagio* is hardly light relief. It is mournful and profound; and the final movement has a raucous solo horn sounding like a car-horn to admonish the solo part in its jaunty and spiky progress. There is a long cadenza for the violin before a sarcastic and striking ending.

Piano Music

Shostakovich wrote a set of *24 Preludes* and a set of *24 Preludes and Fugues*. The *24 Preludes* are short and attractive pieces in the main, with wit and melody to the fore. They are not as progressive as other music he was writing in the early 1930s.

Do listen to the *24 Preludes and Fugues* which are completely different. Inspired by Bach's *Well-tempered Clavier* they are worthy to stand as a 20th century equivalent. They are enormously attractive and riveting pieces, with a great variety of treatment for all the different keys, seen in the calm of *No. 1 in C major*, the whirlwind of *No. 2 in A Minor*, the joy of *No. 3 in G major* and the consolation of *No. 4 in E-Minor*. The set ends with the *D Minor*, a magnificent conclusion, and with Beethoven's spirit never far away. Need I say more?

Chamber Music

Shostakovich found the intimate form of chamber music ideal. It spoke to the heart and performance could be relatively easy to arrange, and private. His series of string quartets, matching the number of symphonies, is unsurpassed in the 20th century.

Before approaching them, however, try the *Piano Quintet*, a profound five-movement work. It opens with the *prelude*, the solo piano setting the stage for a rich string entry. In the following bleak *fugue* we hear a plaintive Russian melody in stark baroque style, gradually opening out then dying away. Shostakovich shows his weird humour in the *scherzo* with a simple melody, bizarre developments and a good sense of fun. The mood changes dramatically for the *intermezzo*, which opens with a long violin threnody, cello pizzicato, like a lament. A further swing in mood brings a happy *finale*, a bolero rhythm entering mid-way to great effect, but the conclusion is gentle.

The Piano Trio No.2 is a riveting work. Its substantial *andante* opens with quiet cello harmonics, in elegiac mood. The *scherzo* is fiercely rhythmic with some great strumming effects, the *largo* – introduced by eight loud chords on the piano is a sad *passacaglia* that leads straight into a *finale* influenced by Shostakovich learning about the Nazi death camps. It is based on a Yiddish melody, graphically played, with swinging pizzicato, building up to a despairing dance of death. At the end we hear the passacaglia theme return and disintegrate.

I think the best way to discover the *String Quartets* is to take them in sequence. It will be a fascinating and rewarding experience. *String Quartet No.1* is highly accessible and short at just 15 minutes in length and, unusually, shows Shostakovich in a positively happy mood! The opening *moderato* has a lovely lilt and a simple melody, the second movement is a set of variations on a Russian theme, cello leading the way. The brief *scherzo* is a buzzing will-of-the-wisp with a lilting *trio* and the *finale* is joyful and playful with a great conclusion.

String Quartet No.2 is much more formidable and three times the length of the first. It opens with a memorable three-note motif whose drama infuses the whole movement. The second movement is titled *Recitative and Romance: Adagio* and the song of the first violin, accompanied by the other strings is highly effective. Next comes *Valse*, dark and brooding before a thrilling *Theme and Variations* that increases in tension and speed before cello and viola break in to sing the theme and lead slowly to its final powerful appearance.

String Quartet No. 3 is considered to be the essence of the composer. In five movements, it too opens directly with a memorable theme, the mood light, the ending witty. Next we are slung into a macabre world by a grotesque waltz, followed by a fierce *allegro non troppo* that sounds orchestral, so rich and loud are the strings. The fourth movement is an *adagio* of great sadness that leads directly into a *finale* that builds to an affirmative great climax before a peaceful dying ending. For your interest the quartet, like several others, has been orchestrated as a chamber symphony and comes across remarkably well in this form.

String Quartet No. 4 has a totally different atmosphere. It is a delightful work in every way, essentially lyrical. A cello drone dominates the opening movement, the following *andantino* is heartfelt and followed by the *allegretto*, playful, fierce and gentle at times. The substantial *finale* opens with a distinctly eastern melody for viola. The overall character is dance-like, slow, deliberate and energetic. The quiet conclusion is enigmatic.

The three-movement *String Quartet No. 5* is one of the most formidable of the series. The opening theme of the first movement is strong and the contrasting lilting second theme is a delight. The middle movement, *andante*, with high strings evokes the eerie sense of stillness that one imagines is outer space. The *finale* introduces a relaxed waltz theme and builds to a formidable climax incorporating themes from all movements before Shostakovich's preferred quiet ending.

String Quartet No. 6 returns to an essentially happy mood with a lilting allegretto, a whimsical moderato con moto, a grave passacaglia in the lento, a dancing, and at times passionate allegretto. All the movements end with the same cadence, a highly original and appealing touch.

String Quartet No. 7 is even shorter than *No. 1*, with a restless first movement, a quiet *lento* where the instruments spin webs around each other, a furious fugue in the *finale* and a weird waltz for a quiet conclusion.

A visit to the city of Dresden, shattered by bombs at the end of World War II, inspired the moving *String Quartet No. 8*, justifiably the most popular of all the quartets. On occasion Shostakovich draws on themes from previous works. The work has five movements, the opening *largo* is laden with grief, the following brilliant *allegro molto* is remorseless and violent and seems to destroy the cultured Mozartean music that appears. Next there is an *allegretto*, a whirling caustic waltz, the main theme from the *Cello Concerto No. 1* appearing. The work concludes with two *largos*, the first dominated by a series of three brutal chords, with a threnody that leads to an exquisite passage for cello based on *Lady Macbeth*. The second *largo* is briefer and despairing.

String Quartet No. 9 is another five-movement work, far removed from the mood of its predecessor in that there is no serious agenda, just the music. The movements run into each other, the moods whimsical, noble, fleeting, eerie, and wild in turn.

String Quartet No. 10 has a relaxed character in all but one of its four movements. A gentle and simple *andante* is followed by an *allegretto furioso*, one of Shostakovich's trademark ferocious scherzos. Next comes a noble *adagio*, in passacaglia form, and an almost playful final movement with lots of pizzicato.

If you have got this far you will not need too much help with the last four quartets. The short and appealing *String Quartet No. 11* is unusual. Written in memory of the second violinist of the Beethoven Quartet who had typically premiered the string quartets, it comprises a suite of seven movements using related themes. The *scherzo* is not the only movement that has unusual and humorous string effects. The *elegy* is the longest movement and the serious one, with the slow movement of Beethoven's *Eroica Symphony* never far away.

String Quartet No. 12 continues Shostakovich's move away from standard structures, being in two movements, with the second three times the length of the first. He also uses 12-tone rows in part. The first movement is quiet and pensive, the second an extraordinarily powerful utterance, with frequent dissonances. Towards the end there is a superb build-up to a climactic and triumphant assertion of major key tonality.

String Quartet No. 13 has one movement of around 20 minutes. It is a bleak work. *String Quartet No. 14* has a prominent role for cello (it was dedicated to the cellist of the Beethoven Quartet). In three movements, the central *adagio* stands out – it also returns to conclude the work. *String Quartet No. 15*, the last, is remarkable in that it consists of six *adagios*. It was written in the last year of his life and is a sad and gloomy masterpiece, profoundly moving at times.

The formidable *Violin Sonata*, written after the *String Quartet No.12*, opens with a profound and uncomplicated *andante*, where the violin holds the melody, with a simple piano accompaniment. The central *allegretto* is an outstanding example of one of Shostakovich's energetic and rhythmic scherzos and the work concludes with a concentrated and substantial *largo – andante* in the form of a passacaglia.

The *Sonata for Cello and Piano, Op.40* is easily accessible. The primary mood of its opening *allegro non troppo* is one of sadness. A brief motorised *allegro* with a trio full of harmonics is followed by a *largo* of great intensity, the cello musing quietly before starting to rhapsodise – intimate and personal. The final *allegro* is sardonic with a pungent development of a Haydn-like theme.

Opera

Shostakovich's great opera *Lady Macbeth of Mtensk* is not dissimilar to that of Janáček's *Katya Kabanová* in story and mood but Shostakovich's opera packs in far more action. It is a brutal story about Katerina Izmailova, the unhappy wife of a Russian provincial merchant, living around 1860. When her husband is called away she takes a lover, Sergei. Her father-in-law, Boris, catches Sergei, beats him and locks him up. Boris, who lusts after Katerina, decides to take advantage of her but she poisons him and frees her lover. Her husband is the next to be murdered. His body is left in her cellar, but is discovered on the day she and Sergei get married. They are arrested, found guilty and sent to Siberia. En route she finds he is after another, younger, female convict, whom she fights in a river. They both drown.

It is a absorbing opera, highly dramatic, the music pungent with a full orchestra, sometimes enormously powerful with brass and percussion, yet often lyrical and delicate. Shostakovich produces extreme contrasts, he sets the moods and covers the action of the different scenes in an extraordinarily effective way. The opening is gentle, lyrical, for Katerina, but soon we have an exciting workers' chorus. The same contrast occurs with the sombre first *Interlude* and the following rushing chorus of labourers tormenting the cook. The music for Katerina alone (e.g. her first bedroom scene) is often beautiful, but it is violent when she and

Sergei consummate their relationship. Later, in another bedroom scene, after intimate music of Mahlerian beauty and intensity, the music for the ghost of Boris could have been written for the Commendatore from Mozart's *Don Giovanni*. The music when Zinovi's corpse is discovered is truly memorable, a macabre and wild dance that continues straight into another *Interlude*. And so this great opera continues inevitably to its tragic end – do try and see it!

With *Volume 4* the *Discovering Classical Music* series continues its exposure of more of the great composers, bringing to life these artists whose music can give so much pleasure. Whilst each volume includes some of the universally recognised geniuses, as the series expands more and more under-rated or under-exposed composers are given Ian Christians' treatment.

A great strength of the series is the even-handedness, each composer is approached in the same way and the same depth whether he is a household name or not. The merit of the composer is not measured by the number of words written about him, each is afforded the space needed to do justice to his life, his personality and his works, but with a conciseness and pithiness for the busy and the curious.

The *Discovering Classical Music* series is thus the exceptional introduction to the subject as is confirmed by its acclaim from an international audience in North America, Australia, South Africa, Europe and Scandinavia.

- "Marvellous", "An ideal introduction", "Pitched perfectly"
- "Glorious", "Wonderful", "Brilliant", "Very rewarding"

APPENDIX

DCM5	DCM6	DCM7	DCM8
1 Albinoni	Palestrina	Byrd	Franck
2 Tallis	Boccherini	Scarlatti	Telemann
3 Paganini	Alkan	Cherubini	Bizet
4 Hummel	Gounod	Grieg	Meyerbeer
5 Bellini	Corelli	Wolf	Webern
6 Donizetti	Holst	Borodin	Rimsky-Korsakov
7 Delius	Glazunov	Mussorgsky	Barber
8 Bruch	Bax	Hindemith	Offenbach
9 Copland	Berg	Poulenc	Saint-Saens
10 Walton	Ives	Schoenberg	Tippett
October 2001	October 2002	October 2003	October 2004

Discovering CLASSICAL MUSIC

1

The lives and music of:
Bach, Mozart, Beethoven, Schubert, Berlioz, Verdi, Bruckner, Dvořák, Tchaikovsky, Mahler

2

The lives and music of:
Vivaldi, Haydn, Mendelssohn, Chopin, Brahms, Elgar, Sibelius, Puccini, Janáček, Rachmaninoff

3

The lives and music of:
Monteverdi, Handel, Rossini, Wagner, Debussy, Nielsen, Vaughan Williams, Richard Strauss, Stravinsky, Prokofiev

FUTURE VOLUMES

5

The lives and music of:
**Albinoni, Tallis, Paganini, Hummel, Bellini,
Donizetti, Delius, Bruch, Copland, Walton**

6

The lives and music of:
**Palestrina, Boccherini, Alkan, Gounod, Corelli,
Holst, Glazunov, Bax, Berg, Ives**

7

The lives and music of:
**Byrd, Scarlatti, Cherubini, Grieg, Wolf, Borodin,
Mussorgsky, Hindemith, Poulenc, Schoenberg**

8

The lives and music of:
**Franck, Telemann, Bizet, Meyerbeer, Webern,
Rimsky-Korsakov, Barber, Offenbach, Saint-Saens, Tippett**

Volumes
of
Discovering Classical Music
are available from
good bookshops and music shops.

In case of difficulty contact:

DCM Publications
1, Hay's Court
133 Rotherhithe Street
London SE16 4NF
Telephone and fax: 020 7231 6944
Email: dcm@orpheusandbacchus.com

Vine House Distribution
Waldenbury, North Common
Chailey
East Sussex BN8 4DR
Telephone: 01825 723398
Fax: 01825 724188